Buy What You Love Without Going Broke

Buy What You Love Without Going Broke

Transform Your Spending and
Get More of What Money Can't Buy

JEN SMITH AND JILL SIRIANNI

HARVEST
An Imprint of WILLIAM MORROW

BUY WHAT YOU LOVE WITHOUT GOING BROKE. Copyright © 2025 by Frugal Friends Podcast LLC. All rights reserved. Printed in the United States of America. No part of this book may be used or reproduced in any manner whatsoever without written permission except in the case of brief quotations embodied in critical articles and reviews. For information, address HarperCollins Publishers, 195 Broadway, New York, NY 10007.

HarperCollins books may be purchased for educational, business, or sales promotional use. For information, please email the Special Markets Department at SPsales@harpercollins.com.

FIRST EDITION

Designed by Jen Overstreet

Library of Congress Cataloging-in-Publication Data has been applied for.

ISBN 978-0-06-337131-6
ISBN 978-0-06-344440-9 (international edition)

24 25 26 27 28 LBC 5 4 3 2 1

For our frugal friends—may you realize you are capable
of greater things.

To Travis—for inspiring me to pursue a life greater than I could've
imagined. And to my boys—for giving my life greater purpose.
—Jen

For Eric—who's been on this journey with me,
making it fun, beautiful, and incredibly worthwhile.
You are my deepest love and the best part of life.
—Jill

Contents

Introduction

Like most good books, we wanted to start this one with a captivating story. But instead, we're going to start it with an email. It's *the* email that changed the course of our lives and set the wheels in motion for the book you're now holding. It came to us from a listener of the *Frugal Friends* podcast who said:

Hi,

I'm just starting out and feel like I'm failing miserably at my frugal journey. Maybe my problem is that I have too much fun buying things. Not just things but experiences too. Recently, you mentioned being frugal can be really fun, but I'd love to know HOW? I have student loan debt, no real savings, and I'm thinking more and more that just owning a home might be an unattainable goal. I love my job as a teacher, but there are no prospects for any significant pay increases so I NEED to be more frugal.

But I also don't want to stop living my life just for the sake of saving. I'm sick of feeling like wanting to shop is a bad thing and that all my financial shortcomings are my fault. I don't think being better at budgeting or buying fewer lattes is the answer, trust me I've tried that. I want to enjoy my life, but I do fear I'm screwing myself over in the long run.

Do you have a podcast episode about ways being frugal is fun, or ways we can make it as fun as buying things is? I've learned so much from you and have put a lot of your advice in place, but I can't say I find being frugal fun. And I need it to be.

Thanks!
Amber

This email highlighted pain points around money so many of us experience. And it challenged us to take a deeper look at some of the difficulties we face in getting the things we want and need while still enjoying our lives. We knew that like Amber, people don't typically see frugality as a fun lifestyle—if anything, it's the opposite. They see it as a lifestyle of deprivation, exploiting resources, and mooching off people. And for years we thought we were addressing this misconception on our podcast by teaching people how to save money on this, spend less on that, and ways to avoid buying home decor. (Here's the best hack: Take it away from its beautifully curated display and look at it next to a trash can to determine if it still looks good in an unaesthetic environment.) But we were looking at the "how," not the "why," and definitely not the "who."

Amber's email served as a reminder that a number in a bank account is a good short-term motivator for cleaning up your spending habits, but it doesn't last. We are people. Not bank accounts. Any real chance we have at achieving our financial goals is going to take time. They say "It's a marathon, not a sprint," but it's way more than a marathon. A marathon is still something that can be run in a day. Financial goals can take decades to achieve. And who wants to live decades without having any fun? The pandemic showed us that you can work hard your whole life to save or build a business and still lose everything due to circumstances outside of your control. So, what's the point in trying so hard? These are the questions our listener was asking. We knew them well because we've asked them too. And when we look to authorities in the world of finance for answers, they all seem to fall short.

Typical personal finance advice has long been a tool that out-of-touch financial experts use to give the rest of us just enough illusion of control that we continue to buy their books and courses and pay them commissions to manage our money for us. But most of the traditional finance advice given is for people who already have money. It's full of math, numbers, and spreadsheets. And any money-saving advice is typically a list of 100+ things to do to save a dollar here and a dollar there. We're told a budget is the solution to all our money problems, and if you can't stick to one, it's not the budget's fault, it's your lack of self-control. If you can't stop eating at restaurants or getting lattes, it's a self-discipline problem, not a time or stress issue. There's always a seven-step program and someone saying "If I can do it, you can too."

But in reality, the math ain't mathin'. And maybe it's because none of these experts had the math teachers we did. Ours always required us to "show your work." In every other class, simply having the answer was enough. Not in math class. Having the answer only provided partial credit, if any. If you wanted full credit, you had to show your work. Sometimes it was frustrating. If I did the work in my head, why did I have to write it all out? If showing my work was essential to getting to the answer, what was the point of the end result? It wasn't until we started reading all these personal finance books and articles that we realized how essential showing your work is. Because we'll admit, when presented with the details of today's economy—student loan debt, underpaid workers, high inflation, and a $700 per month cost of living increase in the last two years—the answer you might be tempted to jump to is "Yeah, forget thriving, surviving will do."

We've spent the last ten years reading and rereading dozens of books on money and psychology. We've interviewed hundreds of personal finance experts on our podcast, *Frugal Friends*, and scoured thousands of articles and studies on everything from budgeting to behavioral economics. We've seen a lot of answers to a lot of questions about spending, saving, and managing money. The common flaw we see in this space is that very few people are showing their work. Figuring out "How do I enjoy life, not feel guilty every time I spend money and not totally screw myself over?" is a simple problem that's deceptively complex to solve. And without context, most people stick to shallow answers that make you feel like you're doing something but are never enough to solve the root problem. Anyone can tell you to stop eating out and take your credit card information out of your computer, but who's really doing that? And if they are, how are they doing it? And is that even the right way? We aim to never give a solution without showing our work. Because there's no singular right solution for managing money or spending it, even if everyone is telling you their way is the right way.

It took us some time to figure out the words to use in response to Amber's email about "making frugal fun." But here's what we said: "Frugality isn't just about shopping less but realizing that shopping isn't what's actually 'fun' or making you happy. It's a temporary dopamine hit that so many other things can provide. The things that make us truly happy cannot be bought. We use frugality to get more of those things. To an extent, the chips are stacked against us and there are very real barriers to affording the things we need and want. Anyone saying anything different is gaslighting. But just because the playing field isn't level doesn't mean we can opt out of the game. Being frugal for frugal's sake is a lifestyle that very few people enjoy. But when you're doing it to get more of what you really love, in a way that works for you, then you'll find the results are very fun."

How we came to this response is the work we intend to show you throughout this book.

Spending Is What We Do, Not Who We Are

When I (Jen) read Amber's email for the first time, I felt like I could've written it. Seven years ago, I couldn't stick to a budget, no matter how high my debt got or how important I knew it was. I'd make a budget that made sense mathematically, but I'd always overspend in one category or another (or all of them). I truly wanted to do better financially, but when it came to spending, I could tell myself no sometimes but not most of the time. And I figured if I couldn't do it right, I might as well stop doing it altogether. Because all budgeting was doing for me was making me feel guilty and childish every time I pulled out my credit card. So, most of the time I'd ignore my savings account and my ever-increasing student loan debt.

Ignoring my financial situation was helpful in that I avoided the crushing weight of anxiety that came with caring. But it was replaced by an underlying anxiety of not knowing what was truly going on. I didn't know how to happily deprive myself, and if wanting to have fun was financially irresponsible, then I'd take it any day over living under a rock. I felt incapable of doing the thing the experts were telling me I should be able to do. I'd spend money, feel guilty, internalize that guilt, and conclude, I'm a "spender." That's what I do, other people are good at saving, I'm good at spending. I don't need to be wealthy. But even when I tried ignoring my debt and tried not to feel guilty about my spending, there was still a twinge of guilt with every purchase I made because I knew I'd never have the feeling of being financially secure.

After several years of this, I met my husband, and in the span of two years we paid off $78,000 of debt and bought a home. I learned that I could stop spending money pretty much altogether. I threw myself into it and took an extreme approach. We didn't eat out, take trips, or buy furniture for the house that was double the size of our apartment. We were living off one salary and putting the entire other salary toward debt. When we decided to buy that house, we saved the down payment in two months (oh, what a time to be a homebuyer!). After two years of bare-minimum spending, I'd become what most people would consider a "saver." With no student loans and a fully funded emergency fund, I thought I was finally good at spending. But instead I found a new problem—hoarding money, saving aggressively, and denying myself the smallest things out of fear I'd need it once it's gone. I still felt like I wasn't doing enough, and I punished myself for wanting more and better. I realized that, even with more income and financial security, the guilt I felt about spending money was not the money's issue. It was mine. And no matter how much I had or how I saw myself financially, nothing would ever be enough. I'd never be able to spend enough or save enough to get what I wanted.

Now when I think of spending, I think of a piece of advice the world was blessed with in 1998 that's aged much better than other advice from the decade. It's from Andy "Brink" Brinker in the Disney Channel original movie *Brink!* In the final skating battle of the movie, he reminds his friends that while they all love skating, "Win or lose, skating is what we do. Not who we are."

We feel the same about spending.

We love the things money can buy us, but at the end of the day, spending is what we do, not who we are.

Our culture puts so much emphasis on what and how you buy to define who you are, but in truth your identity is not tied to what you spend or don't spend on. There is no such thing as being a "spender" or a "saver." Everyone spends, everyone saves. Spending is what we do, not who we are.

If our identities were tied to what we buy, what's the incentive to spend less? Why would we want to be less of who we are? Dinners out, gifts, and traveling the world are great things to spend your money on, but buying them doesn't define who you are or how capable you are with money. In the same vein, a fat bank account, loaded 401(k), and no debt are great, but they too are not the sum of your worth. You can be fun, generous, adventurous, and smart with or without those things.

And you are worthy of all the things you want in life. Not because of the things you buy or don't buy, not in spite of the things you buy or don't buy, but simply because you exist. Not being able to afford something doesn't mean you don't deserve it.

Similarly, your past spending doesn't define who you are now. Credit card debt, student loans, even the hobby you spent hundreds of dollars to start and never ended up doing, these things do not define the kind of spender you are. The spender/saver myth is a lie.

Spending is not a reflection of who you are.

Because spending is a skill.

Spending is a skill because skills can be learned and improved. Sure, there are people who are naturally better at some skills, but even someone less talented can work hard and become better than someone with talent who doesn't hone their skill.

If you've never thought of spending that way, it's not your fault or the fault of those around you for not telling you. Spending isn't taught as a skill—there are no fundamentals classes or specialized seminars. If spending is mentioned in a book, it's usually as a morally ambiguous sidekick to the superior wealth-building strategies of earning and investing (because why learn how to spend when you can just make a ton of money? Everyone can do it!).

Instead, we've been thrust into a world screaming at us to buy who we want to become. As teenagers, we're encouraged to take out an amount of debt for school with no credit check that no young person could get approved for at a Toyota dealership. And without a shred of guidance on how to spend it wisely. How am I supposed to know what costs are worthy of my limited resources?

How many times should I be going out each week?

How much should I spend on groceries?

How many lattes is too many?

How do I save on a car without sacrificing safety?

How do I enjoy takeout without draining my bank account?

How do I buy what I love without going broke?!

Spending money is not the enemy of financial freedom. Spending is essential. It's a skill, not a character flaw. Even homesteaders living off the grid have monthly expenses! And when you separate your spending from your identity and view it as a skill to refine, then you can learn how to practice spending in a way that feels good and completely guilt free.

The Life-Changing Magic of Values-Based Spending

As with any skill, there are sub-skills you can learn to get better. Communication, for example, is an essential life skill. But being able to hold a conversation doesn't automatically make you a great communicator. You also need to improve sub-skills like listening, nonverbal communication, empathy, and confidence. Having money and whipping out a credit card doesn't make you a great spender (despite what capitalism has led us to believe). To improve your spending, you need to brush up on a variety of skills, like problem solving, decision making, creativity, and planning, among others.

And because this collection of skills is so different from the spending you're used to, we made up a whole new name for it: values-based spending.

The goal of values-based spending is to spend without guilt on what you love and build the right barriers to say no to what you don't. It emphasizes finding what matters most to you, on a macro and micro level, and prioritizing spending on or saving for those things. And oftentimes the best way to learn what matters most is to first define the things that don't matter.

With any skill, knowing what to do and how to do it are two different things. It's a simple concept, but simple doesn't mean easy.

When's the last time you sat down and decided what you value? Never? You're not alone. Figuring out what's worth spending on isn't like preferring mint chocolate chip to Grey Poupon ice cream. Defining what you value and don't value is like lining up one hundred delicious ice cream flavors and having to choose your favorites. Every day. There will probably be thirty to forty flavors you like, but some days you can only choose four or five, and other days you'll only be able to pick one, and the one you want most may not be in stock. And as time goes on, your favorites will change for no reason. Life isn't a Baskin-Robbins, but practicing values-based spending will feel a lot like taste testing. In this book, we want to give you the space (and the spoon?) to try new things.

Who Are We? Flattered You'd Ask!

I'm Jen. I'm a wife, mom, and former healthcare professional. I'm passionate about making personal finance accessible to everyone, especially people who don't come from money or families with wealthy connections. I didn't have anyone around to teach me how to earn, invest, or manage my money. The only thing I knew about investing was that my grandmother once invested $2,000 in penny stocks and lost it all. I didn't learn about personal finance until my husband, Travis, and I decided to pay off $78,000 of student loan debt, then did it in two years. It was during those two years that I started sharing what I was learning with friends and family on social media. I started a blog detailing my experiences with side hustles and changing my spending habits, which led to writing about those things for dozens of other personal finance websites, being nominated for several awards, and starting *Frugal Friends Podcast* with my good friend Jill.

Hey, that's me, Jill! Co-owner, cohost and coauthor alongside Jen. I too have no finance degrees, but rather lived experience in identifying what I want from life and leveraging my resources to get it. As a licensed clinical social worker, I have never described my money situation as "robust." I graduated undergrad with $33,000 of student loan debt, which, unfortunately, was more than what I made in a year. My husband, Eric, and I also accumulated other debts, mostly on vehicles, bringing our borrowed total to $60,000. Through nontraditional housing (RV living and house-sitting to name a few), many side hustles, and lots of creativity, we were able to pay it all off and cash-flow my master's degree in seven years. I met Jen on this journey, both of us paying off debt and desiring a safe place to talk about the joys and difficulties of this long-term goal. Our friendship made me wish that lighthearted money conversations with normal people and financial literacy were more accessible, non-shaming, and inclusive. And, so, the podcast was born.

Together we founded *Frugal Friends*, a podcast about saving money where it counts so you can spend freely on what matters. We're not wealth-building gurus and we're not here to upsell you a course or coaching program. We're real-life friends and regular people who've been practicing and fumbling at values-based spending for years. We're not perfect, but we'll share what's worked for us, what hasn't, and why, so you can make the decision to try new things on your journey. In short, we'll show our work. We'll never say "If I can do it, so can you" because we realize everyone's situation is different. We recognize that in many ways we live a privileged life, and some of the hard work that paid off for us five years ago isn't replicable now. So, we aim to share foundational principles that are eternally applicable to as many people in as many life situations as possible. While the principles are unchanging, they can be uniquely applied to any season throughout your life.

How to Master the Skill of Spending Money

If you want to hone your spending skills, it helps to first have a framework for learning a skill in general. We use the Shuhari philosophy. Shuhari is a Japanese martial art concept that describes the stages of learning a skill to mastery, and it helps avoid overwhelm when starting something new.

Shuhari roughly translates to "follow the rules, break the rules, transcend the rules."

Shu means to follow a teacher fully without question. When you're first starting to learn something, whether it be a hobby, language, or spending, you choose one teacher and follow everything they say. There's a lot of conflicting advice in personal finance, and as a beginner you could pull your hair out trying to make sense of it all. So, following one teacher at first can make it easier to put things into practice.

Ha means to break away. Once you have an understanding of basic principles, then you start experimenting with breaking the "rules." If you study famous artists, you can usually see this visually over the body of their works. Once they get comfortable with their teacher's style, they start to innovate and develop their own style based on it. You can start to disagree with authors, influencers, and podcasters whose desires, lifestyle, and season are different from yours. Again, you'll never find a perfect teacher. No expert's life or choices are going to fully line up with yours, that's why it's good to have multiple teachers. Find a collective wisdom from a variety of experts who help you keep moving in the right direction.

Ri means to transcend. At this stage you've "mastered"—not perfected—your skill. You'll never be a perfect spender, or perfect at anything for that matter, but at this point you've earned the right to be confident and make your own rules. It's important to get to this stage but not to rush it. People who pretend to be there too soon can lead themselves (and others) down a potentially destructive path. But people who avoid it risk being swayed by "shiny object syndrome" whenever an influencer has a new viral financial hack.

When my husband, Travis, and I (Jen) were paying off our debt, we listened to an expert who said you should get out of debt as quickly as possible and you shouldn't spend money on anything nonessential until you're out of debt. It was extreme, and there were positives and negatives to living that lifestyle. On one hand, I felt miserable missing out on so many things that cost money, but on the other it forced me to get creative in meeting my "wants." I found free ways to get what I wanted that I would've never thought of without the strict rule, and it taught me foundational lessons about what I value. Eventually I started listening to other teachers who were more lax on debt payoff and were, as a result, more lax on spending while paying off debt. I even listened to a few who loved debt and praised its merits. We started *Frugal Friends* to share all these new viewpoints and how we were, and weren't, using them. As we recorded more episodes and studied more perspectives, we created our own rules for spending and found that if we wanted to spend guilt free (without sacrificing ourselves to the corporate ladder), we had to spend on what we value.

One of the reasons we think there's so much guilt associated with spending is that most financial experts explain their methods as if they're the best and only course of action. And anyone who deviates is doing it wrong. But we're here to tell you that just because you follow a financial expert and respect how they spend and save, it doesn't mean you have to practice your spending the exact same way to be successful. Improving spending is going to look different for everyone. That's why figuring out who to learn from, how to learn it, and what's best for you is so important.

There are a lot of places to go for financial education. Books are the number one place to start (look at you already on the right track!). It can be hard to know what teachers to trust, but a lot of work goes into a book and there are a lot of people who read it before it goes to print and review it after, so you can go into a book with a decent level of trust in what the author's saying. Podcasts are another good place (shameless plug for *Frugal Friends Podcast*!). Are we biased? Sure. But a podcast does give you access to teachers for hours upon hours, and you can quickly decide for yourself if a teacher is right for you or not. Then there's social media and YouTube. These are great for getting information but not great for assessing the creators' accuracy or trustworthiness. These platforms are driven by algorithms that reward content for how many clicks and views they get, not by how correct or helpful the information is. There are some amazing educators on these platforms—you just have to be careful and do extra vetting outside of them.

On your values-based spending journey, you'll learn from a variety of people. Some will help you spend better, others will help you earn more and learn how to invest it. There is no expert who meets every need for every person. We all need a variety of teachers so we can be sure we're learning the right skills at the right time.

Spending in the Radical Middle

There's nothing worse than when a book gives all this advice that makes total sense in the author's perfect made-up book world but doesn't apply it to the real world, where life is nuanced. You may value one thing over another, but if the lesser is more urgent, what do you choose? You may value something but not be in a season to buy it. What do you spend on, then? The "buy nothing" and "buy everything" extremes are much easier to maintain because the decisions are made for you. But when you reject the extremes at either end of the spectrum, you find the middle.

People glorify extremes in books and on the internet, and they capitalize on them. On one end of the internet, people are saying "Spend as little as possible, pay off debt as quickly as possible, and retire as early as possible!" On the other end, they're saying "Saving is pointless, buy what you want, when you want it!" or "Anyone can make a million dollars a year in my proven real estate investing pyramid scheme team." Extremes get the most attention—it's why they go viral on social media. And while we're not against familiarizing yourself with everything that's out there, the all-or-nothing approach is a skill-learning killer. If you want to learn the skills needed to practice values-based spending, you have to transcend the noise of extremes, embrace the nuance, and find your place in the middle. Looking for your middle instead of living in the extremes is a radical concept that, while unlikely to go viral, will help you get the most out of your journey. In a world that loves extremes, finding your place in the middle is radical. And the radical middle is at the core of values-based spending.

With everything our brains have to process at any given moment, especially as we learn new topics, sometimes it is easier to be told what to think. It's why we start learning a skill with just one teacher. We're naturally attracted to the all-or-nothing" methods because absolute right and wrong choices are easier to process.

The radical middle isn't the rejection of extremes, it's holding the tension between them. It refuses to believe that there are only two sides and looks for the middle ground or a third option. It forces creativity, empathy, and forgiveness in a world that says "My way or the highway." When you reject the either/or binary and replace it with both/and, you open yourself up to living a life that's fully your own, not one that someone else has designed for you.

Throughout the rest of this book, you'll learn how to master the skill of spending and how to find your radical middle when your situation may be different from ours. We'll dive deeper into the mindset shifts and action steps you can take to find what you love, say no to what you don't, and, ultimately, not go broke. And we've divided the book into those aptly named sections.

In part 1, we'll talk about how to buy what you love. You'll learn how to identify what you love spending on, the things money can't buy, and how to find the radical middle between the two. One of the foundational sub-skills to values-based spending is healthy communication . . . with yourself. We'll go in depth on where to focus your attention and how to speak to yourself when you're making spending decisions, and what to do when you make a decision you're not proud of. We'll also cover what to do when decision-making isn't simple, like when you're in a season of life that doesn't allow for certain things, or how to prioritize your values when you can't afford them all.

In part 2, we'll focus on how to say no. This is something most books stop short of or never touch on, but we're devoting three whole chapters to it. We'll start by covering why you can't stop spending and why that's intentional. We'll talk about dopamine as a factor in making shopping addictive, how to reset your dopamine receptors, and the psychology behind various reasons why you spend. Then we'll wrap up with how to stop overspending on the things you can't avoid entirely.

In part 3, we tell you how to avoid going broke, which is essentially practical tips to make all this sustainable so you can stick with it long enough to master the skill. We'll look at your zones of influence so you can set up your environments, internally and externally, for success.

In each part, our aim is to show our work. You won't leave a chapter without knowing how to take action, and why each action is recommended so you don't waste your time with things that will never work for you. Each chapter will end with a lightning-round question and an action step. On the podcast, we call the lightning round our vulnerability segment. At the end of each episode, we share a real-life peek into our lives and the radical middle we're finding between knowing what we're supposed to do and actually doing it. Each lightning-round question in this book will give you the opportunity to do the same. Get honest about your answers to these questions and you'll be a step closer to honing your values-based spending skills. The action step will give you one thing to do or show you how to take action based on what you just read. It's not a requirement to complete before you move on, but we invite you to start implementing these practices when you're ready. You will hear from both of us (Jen and Jill) throughout the book—we each wrote different chapters and sometimes we pop up in each other's chapters—but we will be sure to let you know who's talking.

Let's Go

No matter where you are, what you earn, or what you love, you can improve your spending. In fact, we believe your biggest barrier to learning values-based spending will not be your capacity for learning a new skill, it will be your hesitance to unlearn the ideas that you don't need to spend money to become who you want to be. You don't need to buy people things to be loving, you don't need to buy your kids stuff to be a good parent, you don't need to buy items to support causes, and you don't need to buy new clothes to be accepted or taken seriously. You can spend money to have fun, but you don't need to.

We're so excited to be with you on this journey. And it is a lifelong journey. Mastery of a skill is not a destination. We're going to do everything in our power to help you, but we can't fight the battle for you. You're going to be the one in the store or on the website, making the final decision to buy now or forever hold your peace. And we know you are more than capable. Be encouraged, you don't have to get it right every time, your path doesn't have to look like anyone else's, and any step in the right direction IS A STEP IN THE RIGHT DIRECTION!

So, if you're ready to start this journey of shedding the consumer identity the world has given you, bucking the trend of sedative consumption, and finally feeling good about your finances, then let's go. You're about to learn new things about an old subject that are going to change the way you shop, transform the way you spend, and make you a pro at saving money!

Forget what you thought you knew about spending and prepare to buy what you love without going broke.

⚡ Lightning Round ⚡

Have you ever tied your spending to your identity? Do you think it's held you back from improving the way you spend?

Action Step

Head to frugalfriendspodcast.com/book to download the free resources for the book. You'll get access to templates, video examples, and recommendations to help you master the most important concepts in the book!

PART 1

Buy What You Love

CHAPTER 1

What Is Love?

In 2011, Tom Haverford and Donna Meagle introduced us to a concept that would change a generation forever:

Treat Yo Self.

Not familiar? Once a year Donna and Tom spend a day, specifically October 13th, treating themselves. What do they treat themselves to?

Clothes? Treat Yo Self!
Fragrances? Treat Yo Self!
Massages? Treat Yo Self!
Mimosas? Treat Yo Self!
Fine. Leather. Goods?
Treat. Yo. Self.
It's the best day of the year.

Even if you didn't watch the series *Parks and Recreation*, you've probably heard the phrase "Treat Yo Self." While we all love that monologue, we love what happens at the end of the episode even more. Tom and Donna invite Ben, their uptight coworker, to partake in Treat Yo Self Day. Ben has a hard time relaxing, and after a day full of pampering and shopping, all he's "treated" himself to is a bag of socks, which infuriates Tom. Donna, in her transcendent wisdom, reasons with Tom that maybe this version of Treat Yo Self Day works for them and maybe Ben needs his own version. She asks Ben if he could blow big money on one thing—not sock money—what would it be? He thinks about it for a TV minute, and the camera cuts to him walking out of a dressing room . . . in a movie-quality Batman costume.

The path to figuring out what you love to buy is lifelong. But it starts and continues with asking yourself a lot of questions, like if you could blow big money, not sock money, on one thing, what would it be? The tricky part is, most of the time, the things we actually want to buy aren't fine leather goods or superhero costumes. They're hard to pin down because they don't have concrete price tags.

Your Needs, My Needs

When we think about buying what we love, there are two categories: the tangible and the intangible. The tangible things are what people think of first: lattes, dinners, plane tickets. The intangible are the things we want but are harder to place a price tag on (even though there is a financial component to getting them): time with family and friends, health, and self-fulfillment. If we asked you what's more important, tangible or intangible things, you'd probably say the intangible. Most people do. So why is it that they're not the things we think of first when we consider what we spend "big money" on?

Maybe it's because we've been taught that "love don't cost a thing" and "the best things in life are free." If you've spent any time in this post-Covid world, you know those are both false. Personally, we think "I don't want no scrub" and "Cash rules everything around me" are more accurate mantras. Because the less money you have, the harder it is to pursue the intangibles you want.

Another reason might be that we've been taught that in order to look like we "have it together," we have to keep up with the purchases, trends, and home renovations of everyone else. The world is constantly telling us we need to buy things to express who we are. People judge how we're doing based on our appearance and how clean our home is on social media. (Pro tip: You only ever need to clean ten square feet of your home on a rotating basis to make everyone on social media think your whole home is spotless all the time!) When we desire the approval of others or want people to have a good perception of us, it's easier to gain this through our purchases than to explain the internal things that are fulfilling us. Buying things, wanting things, and loving tangible things is not bad. We've just gotten a little lost in how we prioritize them with the intangible things money can't directly buy. Because the intangible are not just things we want, they're things we need.

We think of needs as just the necessities for physical survival, but many of our internal desires are needs as well. We obviously need to meet physical needs first, but once our physical needs are met, our brains want more and move on to these higher internal needs. And the more our society focuses on buying tangible items as the way to meet all our needs, the further we get from the well-rounded health our brains are after.

We're consuming goods at a higher rate, but we're not getting happier. In a 2024 Gallup poll, 29 percent of US adults reported having been diagnosed with depression at some point in their lifetime, nearly 10 percent higher than in 2015, and the rate of anxiety among eighteen- to twenty-five-year-olds nearly doubled from 2008 to 2018. When you don't treat internal desires as needs, they don't just go away. Regardless of how you value them, you will blatantly or subconsciously pursue them, and oftentimes that means spending on them.

I (Jen) used to love going out with friends. I would go out four to six times a week for dinner, coffee, or happy hour. I had never given myself space to think about why I loved going out. But when Travis and I committed to paying off our debt and I stopped eating out as much, I was forced to think about it. I realized it wasn't the food and drinks I missed, it was the people. When I figured that out, I recognized that going out wasn't even the best way to spend meaningful time with friends. Most of the time the restaurants were loud, the chairs were far apart, and our mouths were full. I spent all that money and rarely got what I really wanted, which just led to more spending on it because the true need wasn't being met. And not only was I not meeting the need, the spending led to guilt because it was outside of traditionally defined "needs."

The tension between physical and internal needs isn't new. In 1943, psychologist Abraham Maslow explained our diverse range of internal and external desires as a "hierarchy of needs." He recognized that while some needs are more important than others, as in your body literally cannot function without some of them, others are necessary in order to function well. Maslow's hierarchy of needs is aptly depicted as a triangle divided into five levels. We've included our favorite depiction of it on the resources page for this book available at www.frugalfriendspodcast.com/book. Our most basic needs are at the base: physiological needs like food, water, and shelter. Above that come the needs that aren't tangible but are still deemed essential: Safety needs like health, employment, and physical security. The third and fourth levels are psychological needs like love and a sense of belonging, followed by self-esteem. This is where society starts to mistake needs for wants. And at the tippy-top is the need that generally gets taken for granted: self-fulfillment, the feeling that you are meeting your full potential. Maslow's theory says that lower-level basic needs must be met before we can pursue higher-level needs. It's why so much of the conversation around spending money is confined to tangible stuff. But once we meet those lower-level basic needs, and even if they're not met 100 percent, our brains move on to wanting to achieve the higher-level needs, no matter how limited our income. I don't know about you, but there have been many times I've "overspent" my budget to buy a self-help book or because a friend wanted to get dinner. It wasn't because I needed the book or the dinner—my basic needs had been met. I was pursuing higher-level needs.

And suppressing our higher-level, internal needs can cost us more than money. We all know people who've stayed in bad relationships because they don't know their worth and people-pleasers who overextend themselves.

For at least the last one hundred years, we've been told that our worth as a person is tied to how many physical and safety needs we can accumulate. As a result, we are very blatantly judged by, and spend more on, our home, cars, vacations, and how "healthy" we look while neglecting things like relationships and self-fulfillment.

It's not ideal, but the other extreme isn't the answer either. People who pursue a sense of belonging and self-actualization above foundational needs won't get what they want unless what they want is to end up in a cult documentary on HBO.

So, in your quest to figure out what you love, know that your first loves probably aren't things per se, but more like needs, both external and internal. And similar to Maslow's triangle, what you love won't be linear but more of a hierarchy. Because you can't find purpose on an empty stomach.

What Money Can't Buy

When we started paying off debt I (still Jen) immediately cut out happy hours, restaurants, and other high-cost activities with friends. And I was, to no one's surprise, miserable.

The problem with trying to cut out dinners and coffees for the sake of cutting costs is that you're also cutting out whatever reason you had for buying those things. Unless you identify what you're truly after, you'll keep spending to acquire things that money can't buy.

When I examined my needs and found that relationships were at the core of why I was going out, I was able to get creative in how I met the need, instead of immediately buying the quick fix. But it took time to get there.

It might be why some of your prior attempts at "controlling" your spending didn't last long or left you saying, "Why do I keep over-spending when I don't want to?" When I identified what I was after, I started looking for ways to pursue it that didn't cost me money. I invited friends over for wine nights or a potluck, we attended free movies in the park, or brought our coffees to the playground.

The first principle of values-based spending and buying what you love is knowing that the things we love most can't be bought. And since that's a very abstract thing to say, we like to give it some spec-ificity by naming a few things that we and almost all our listeners have stated are their highest values. And they are all conveniently F words.

We call them the four F's: **family**, **friends**, **faith**, and **fulfilling work**. You can absolutely add your own (bonus points if it's another F word), but these are the internal needs that we've found most im-portant to us and that have been echoed throughout the studies we've read.

Like in a Pew Research study where two separate surveys were ad-ministered that asked the same question: What makes your life feel meaningful, fulfilling, or satisfying? The first poll was open-ended, meaning respondents could enter anything. The second was closed, meaning respondents could only choose from a list of fifteen possible sources. It also asked which of these sources gave respondents the most meaning and fulfillment. Across both surveys, the most popular an-swer was clear and consistent: Family gave life the most meaning and fulfillment. After that, respondents had many answers, but there were four that came up at or near the top of both surveys: career, money, faith, and friends. A lot of the open-ended responses about money were directly related to career and a lot of career responses mentioned feeling purpose or enjoying their career. We know that relationships, job security, self-worth, and fulfillment are all important thanks to Maslow's hierarchy of needs. But what does each of these 4 F's mean for our finances?

Just like the survey's conclusion, **family** is also what we hear from our listeners as what they value most. And it's what we value most in our lives too! More than anything, we want more time and deeper relationships with our partners, kids, siblings, and parents. Well, some parents more than others. Relationships are so vital to maintaining values-based spending that we've devoted a whole chapter to them later in the book. That's because, when healthy, relationships with family and friends keep us motivated. They're also the best way to meet our connection and intimacy needs and our higher needs, like self-esteem and respect. When unhealthy, they can deplete these needs as fast as they fill them. When it comes to money, we think there's no better place to spend than on family. Whether that's on a vacation to spend quality time or simply buying a gratuitous number of monster truck toys to incentivize a three-year-old's potty-training efforts. We've also both joyfully helped family members financially in times of need. In addition to the money we'd gladly spend, there are expenses for our family that aren't as fun but that we are responsible for, like extra equipment and tournaments for a child who's exceptionally good at sports or providing financial support for a parent who's ill. Because there are so many expenses that are good and necessary, sometimes we can rationalize that all expenses for our family are good or necessary. I know I've paid for lessons my kids didn't want and dinners my husband didn't enjoy because I thought that's what I had to do to be a good mom and wife. And nowhere are financial boundary lines crossed more than within families where pressure and coercion can influence spending. A huge part of spending in alignment with your values will be figuring out the difference between the expenses you'll gladly pay for your family and the ones you need to build boundaries to avoid.

Friends are our community outside of family, and at times our chosen family. Lack of time, past traumas like broken trust, and an ever-dividing country have made finding friends difficult, but friendship remains at the core of our being. Another Pew Research Center survey found that 69 percent of Americans have three or more close friends and 38 percent of those have more than five. They also found that having more friends is linked to being more satisfied with those friendships. (Because no woman can do it all, amiright?) I (Jen) find that the older I become and the more kids I have, the harder it gets to maintain friendships. And while my five-year-old says I'm his best friend, we have vastly different interests. There are seasons in life when we get to prioritize friendships more highly than others. Part of values-based spending is knowing when you're in one of those seasons and embracing it (another topic we'll get into soon). It's also about knowing when to shift. Some friendships are long-term, but many are given to us for shorter seasons. When I stopped going out, I gave up some friendships with people who were more interested in going out than building relationships. But I've picked up others, like moms who also lack the interests of their five-year-old boys. As we get more creative with meeting our needs of friendship and belonging in a way that fits our budget, we naturally fall into places with like-minded people. It's okay to grieve the loss of relationships that were good and be thankful for new relationships that are healthier for where we're going.

Next is **faith**, a subject we understand brings up unique feelings depending on who you ask. Whether your spiritual practice is organized, organic, or a combination of both, we believe having one is essential to all our internal needs, primarily self-actualization. Learning, volunteering, meditation, prayer, journaling, and spending time in nature are all ways we can connect to our greater purpose and make sense of a world too complex to fully understand. And generosity, whether to a church or organization you love, has been reported to have strong associations with psychological health and well-being. An intentional spiritual practice can also make us more mindful of the spaces around us. It can even allow us to see our homes as a personal sanctuary where we can reflect and recharge. When you value your spiritual practice, things like limiting your consumption (and thereby your clutter), investing in the right home-improvement projects, and spending mindfully aren't just money-saving ideas, they're value-aligned actions.

Finally, we have **fulfilling work**. The great thing about fulfilling work is that it shouldn't cost anything, it should pay you! (A great phrase to use on the next girl boss trying to recruit you for her network marketing business!) Fulfilling work covers a variety of internal and external needs: the security of a paycheck, confidence, achievement, creativity, and more. A few years ago, my husband, Travis, was working a job that would constantly call him in at all hours of the night and weekend, far beyond the forty hours he put in every week. When he told me he wanted to take a $20,000 pay cut to work a job with no nights, no on-call, and didn't require us to move, I was . . . eventually . . . all for it. Because we weren't spending on the edge of what we were earning, it was a change we could afford to make. Fulfilling work doesn't have to mean a pay cut, though it is great to have enough financial security to be able to choose it. And our hope is that this job can expand his skill-set and lead to an even higher paying job opportunity in a few years. Sometimes we do spend in order to pursue fulfilling work, which can result in increased income. Earning a degree or investing in skill improvement can lead to raises, promotions, and new job opportunities in what you're already doing or in a completely new field. We've also seen people save a year's salary to go full-time in a side business that's starting to take off. We like to shed light on this aspect of different ways we may pursue fulfilling work or what our careers might look like because so much personal finance advice regarding income is one-sided. It's all "earn more." It's endless talk about charging what you're worth, negotiating, asking for more, job hopping for raises, and while all of that is good and useful, it's not always the best route or doable in certain seasons. Sometimes the right move is earning more and other times it's taking the pay cut or sacrificing a raise for a job you like in a location you love. While both are OK, we don't want you to leave this book thinking that you either *have* to earn more or that you *can't* earn more. You can decide if a pay raise, a pay cut, or pay maintenance is best for you and what you want from life. And, of course, if you feel your compensation doesn't match the effort you put in or that you have more to give and you want to be compensated appropriately for it, then you can improve it and you should be looking for opportunities to improve it.

As a social worker, I (Jill) experienced this firsthand. While in many ways my career provided purpose, early on I held roles that were incredibly depleting both emotionally and financially because I thought that was my lot in life as a result of the field I'd chosen. I was serving as a clinical case manager for at-risk youth in a group home working sixty hours a week for $24,000 a year. I was underpaid and overworked in every sense of the phrase. I knew the organization was suffering financially, and I thought it was my duty to sacrifice earning a livable wage for the sake of the teens I cared for deeply. I thought that I couldn't ask to be compensated more and that no other place would give me more. Until I was finally able to reject the "either/or" options and find my radical middle of *both* fulfilling social justice work *and* reasonable compensation. I was able to increase my income by $31,000 a year in a matter of three years. This was made possible by two job changes and earning my master's degree within that time. Those decisions led me to finding an organization with practices that matched their ethos; they cared for all people, including their employees, and compensated us fairly. I didn't have to leave the field I loved, I just needed to get creative with how I engaged in fulfilling work.

If your income isn't covering the basics, you're not going to be able to pursue any needs beyond physical and every financial move you make is going to feel stressful. So instead of viewing either earning more or living on less as better than the other, finding your radical middle and values-based spending can support you wherever you choose to land.

The four F's are going to look different for everyone, but they are the baseline for figuring out what you love and where you want to spend your money. If you know what you want most is to be able to pick your kids up from school every day without being beholden to a 9 to 5 schedule, you will spend your time better (probably looking for a new job or starting your own business), you will spend your money better (saving to be able to quit), and you will make more strategic goals (like avoiding a brand-new car purchase or paying off debt to lower your monthly expenses). If you don't know what you're really after, then leaving your job just looks like one of the hundreds of good ideas that seem out of reach. And if it's out of reach, might as well buy a latte every afternoon to reward yourself for dealing with your horrible boss who won't let you pick your kids up! *So, before you think about the tangible things you love to buy, invest time in thinking about how to afford the things you want that money can't buy.* Think about how much time you'd like to spend with your family and what kind of work schedule you need to do it. Think about how you'd like to show up as a partner, parent, and friend. And think about how you want to disconnect from the noise of the world and connect more intentionally to what's significant. When you think about things like these, values-based spending isn't just a way to save money or spend without guilt. It becomes your gateway to living a values-aligned life.

Money Also Can't Buy This

Before we move on to the tangible things, let's talk about one more intangible.

I (Jen) have got a lot to thank Kim Kardashian for.

When *Keeping Up with the Kardashians* premiered in 2007, having curves was not cool. However, by the time I'd graduated college, Kim had made a delicious derriere the hot thing to have. People were buying glute-focused workout routines, butt-beautifying products, and pants designed to give the optical illusion of a butt. Not me. I am naturally blessed. And in my early twenties, I needed something about my body to be proud of.

Because my entire life I'd been told I was overweight. I was big around the hips, not naturally athletic, and definitely not the ideal of late '90s/early 2000s physique. With two low-income working parents, my family didn't have a lot of money or the time needed to prepare healthy foods, and even if they did, their parents never taught them how or knew it was important themselves. My parents wouldn't directly tell me I was fat, it was always phrased as "We need to lose some weight." They projected their insecurities on me, and I internalized them. My mom would buy diet pills and whatever the newest "As seen on TV" diet fad was, but all I got was my pediatrician telling my mom to stop giving me whole milk. Toward the end of college, I decided to do something about it. I started running. I ran a half marathon, and once I got a full-time job and some disposable income, I joined CrossFit. I started to fall in love with what my body could do, but I never stopped feeling insecure about it. I was in a good place for a while, then I had kids. My body supported the growth of two human beings, delivered them safely, and then had the nerve to not return to the shape from whence it came. I felt betrayed. I wish, after two healthy babies and six half marathons, I could say I've worked through my body issues, but I'm not there yet. I am still scrolling fitness accounts on social media with "before and after" shots. For me it's always a before, never an after. And no matter how much money I've spent to feel good about my body, it's never been enough. I've never been able to buy that love, and neither can you. But it doesn't stop many of us from trying.

In 2022, the US weight-loss market was valued at $135.7 billion. Every year Americans' spending on supplements, meal replacements, fitness equipment, weight-loss programs, and surgical procedures like liposuction and gastric bypass surgery outpaces inflation. And despite the growing body positivity movement (which is now just a marketing tactic to sell you products to "love" your body more), Ozempic, known generically as semaglutide, was Science.org's 2023 Breakthrough Drug of the Year.

Prescriptions for weight-loss drugs serve a necessary purpose on the market. But prescriptions for them have skyrocketed over the past five years. Semaglutide's prescription rate nearly doubled in 2023 alone, while its competitor tirzepatide (Mounjaro and Zepbound) rose 141 percent. By the end of the year, all people could talk about was which of the injectables could help you lose weight faster. Without insurance, one dose of Ozempic retails for over $900. The media reported that the only limit to how much these drug companies could earn was how fast they could crank them out. The industry is fueled by insecurities that knows its profits are driven by the fact that we don't love ourselves as we are.

Ozempic isn't the first diet craze to turn a profit from our insecurities, and it won't be the last. You can replace "diet" with any product or service that manipulates natural and good desires. The beauty industry, skin-care industry, fashion industry, even the food industries are all guilty of manipulating our collective self-consciousness.

I was able to tell people my expensive gym membership and shipments of protein and pre-workout powders were because I wanted to be healthy, and while that wasn't a lie, I knew it wasn't the whole truth. I didn't love my body, and I was spending real money to solve a manufactured problem.

Figuring out if you love something enough to buy it is a bumpy ride. You'll get it right sometimes, but you'll get it wrong a lot, especially at first. But there's nothing you can buy, no outfit, organizer, planner, health craze, beauty procedure, trip, or experience that will make you good enough to love yourself if you don't already. Until you choose to love yourself as you are, you will keep spending to gain your own approval. And in the end, with little to no savings, all you'll be left with is another reason to be disappointed in yourself.

The sooner you realize that money can't buy you who you want to be, the faster you'll be able to figure out the things you love to buy because *you* love them. Not because of some made-up standard of beauty, career, parenting, or whatever. But because they matter to you, and you are valuable.

⚡ **Lightning Round** ⚡

How do you want to show up in your family, friendships, faith, and fulfilling work? Where do you need to disconnect from the noise of the world to connect more intentionally to what's significant?

⚠

Action Step

Write down one thing in each category (family, friendships, faith, and fulfilling work) that you need to buy, save for, or stop spending on in the next six months to get you closer to your values-aligned life.

CHAPTER 2

But I Love Everything

If you've listened to our podcast for any amount of time, you know how much I (Jill) love my nieces and nephews. I live far from them, so visiting is one of my deepest joys. We have so. much. fun. Mostly because I don't need to worry about sleep schedules, nutritional content of food, or anything related to behavior modification. We go on walks, skip rocks, pick flowers, eat snacks, and play "taco"—a game we made up where I try to catch them and roll them in a blanket like a taco. It's wild. And hilarious. And someone always gets hurt (usually me). In the midst of all these shenanigans, something that continues to strike me about these kiddos is their unrelenting curiosity. It shows up in each one of them a bit differently, but they are all so genuinely curious about the world around them.

For Jack, my four-year-old nephew, curiosity showed up through his fascination with slugs. As it turns out, the backyard was full of them, and he was on a mission to collect them all. He had no reservations about picking them up, and we quickly learned that the slime of slugs is nearly impossible to get off skin, but that didn't deter him. He was so intrigued by those little mollusks, and with every newfound slug there were newly formed questions: "What's that one doing? Why is he so small? Is this his home? Where's his mom? Can we go look for more, Aunt Jill?" I had no answers to his questions except for that last one: "Jack, do you think we could just look at the snails you already found?" "But I love them ALL!" he pleaded. Truthfully, I understood.

I want all the good things too. Maybe not snails, but there's a lot of cool stuff I love and want. Like dinners out, multiple vacations a year, a paid-off car, affordable housing, excellent medical coverage, fully funded retirement accounts, top-shelf skin-care products, and if we're really shooting for the moon, let's throw in a pool!

For Jack, his curiosity about what's hiding under damp logs led him to want more and more of that thing. And this is the propensity for us all. When you first think about buying what you love without going broke, you may be thinking, there are a lot of things I love, and I want to know how to afford them all! It's where we all start. You want to love everything and be able to say yes to all of it, and when you can't, you think it's a money problem or a "you" problem.

Unfortunately, Jack couldn't have all the slugs hiding in the woods that day, and I still don't have great medical coverage or a pool. But I learned something from his adorable (and slightly gross) approach to discovering the world around him. He was genuinely curious about these slimy creatures, and while his version of curiosity led to extreme slug hoarding, our version can help us refine our list of what we love. We often try to find what we value by getting curious about the things we can buy, but truly finding what you value actually comes from getting curious about yourself.

Practicing curiosity comes quite naturally to kids because they have so much to discover about themselves, the people they love, and the greater world around them. We can lose sight of this ability by adulthood and forget to approach our circumstances with this posture. We think we've got a pretty good grasp on knowing ourselves, only to find that the things we "know" are a combination of things we've picked up or been influenced by along the way, and some of it may not actually fit us.

But what would it look like if we made efforts to take on a "not-knowing" posture? I'm not talking about playing dumb, but rather actively rejecting assumptions. This would also mean approaching our various circumstances without pretending to know the future, what's going to happen next, or thinking that we know the meaning of each occurrence, decision, or behavior—of others or ourselves!

If I've learned anything from my nieces and nephews, it's that curiosity is aimed at discovery and not assuming what might be found. Curiosity comes with more questions than answers and includes exploration. Sometimes curiosity is satisfied and sometimes it leads to more curiosity. But the best version of curiosity is the kind that doesn't already know the answers, isn't laced with coercion or ulterior motives, and truly wants to know and unearth the truth.

When we're able to train ourselves to be curious, we are better able to navigate our circumstances with decreased judgment and less shame. What this means for our finances is increased knowledge of self and ability to bring our spending into alignment with that knowledge. When curiosity is our launching point, we have greater potential to truly understand the inner workings of ourselves and the world around us in a manner that allows us to feel confident about the spending and savings decisions we make.

I use the concept of curiosity very often in my work in the mental health field. Over the years I have engaged with countless individuals ranging in age from eight to eighty-two, each from a variety of backgrounds and each journeying through numerous and varied difficulties. Something nearly everyone (including myself) had in common was judgment toward self. While we are the experts on ourselves, that doesn't mean we always view ourselves entirely accurately. Inevitably we all possess some number of "cognitive distortions," or said more plainly, "unhelpful thinking styles." These can include mindsets like:

Labeling. This is when we sum up ourselves with an overarching statement, like "I'm hopeless" or "I'm just a hot mess." We can adopt these narratives and believe we'll never change. In addition to people referring to themselves as a "spender" or a "saver," we've received countless emails over the years from people saying things like "I've made too many mistakes to recover" or "I'm too old to pay off debt."

They're willing to renounce themselves to a subpar life because of a label they accepted as part of their identity.

Overgeneralizing. This is when we identify a pattern based on not enough data. We usually anchor our bias to the first few facts we get about a new topic whether or not those facts are backed up by others or long-term data. Like believing budgeting doesn't work because your first few budgets didn't work or that the stock market is rigged because it happened to be in a bear market when you invested.

Catastrophizing is when we view or think about situations disproportionately, often attributing "terrible," "horrible," "awful" conclusions not congruent with reality. Like the time I got a letter from the IRS saying I still owed all my taxes from the previous year that I *knew* I already paid. I immediately assumed the next thing to show up at my door would be a police officer taking me straight to jail. In reality, I just had to prove again that I already paid my taxes. It was annoying, but I didn't get locked up for life. Catastrophizing can also cause us to hoard money because of all the bad things that could happen if we spend it or do the opposite and spend it all out of fear we won't get it again.

Should-ing and must-ing. This is highly intertwined with our own unreasonable expectations of ourselves. We think "I *should* be able to stop ordering takeout" or "I *must* pay off my debt as quickly as possible." When we can't live up to these self-imposed pressures, we are left with feelings of shame, guilt, or frustration.

All-or-nothing. This involves viewing things or evaluating ourselves in an "all good" or "all bad" manner, unwilling to accept ambiguity or "gray" areas. It's this type of thinking that keeps us from the radical middle. And many times, the "all-or-nothing" is completely arbitrary. We make up standards for how we should spend, and when we don't meet them, we give up on the bigger goal entirely. This is what has halted many of our friends from investing for their retirement. If they couldn't max out their Roth IRA or didn't have an employer offering a 401(k), it didn't feel worth it to them.

This list is not exhaustive, but it can help you understand your thinking patterns and how you rationalize your thoughts about and actions with spending. And with any one of these unhelpful thinking styles, curiosity is the best place to begin. When it comes to your behaviors around money, any one (or combination) of these unhelpful thinking styles may be at play. When you notice yourself catastrophizing your debt or minimizing the importance of caring about the future, you can simply ask what that thinking pattern is connected to. Or what from your experience is causing you to believe, reason, or act in this way. These questions allow you to get to the core issue and have greater success in implementing an informed response that targets the root.

Barriers: What's in the Way of Curiosity?

Self-reflection can be difficult and often doesn't come naturally. We have years (for some of us decades!) of life experiences, patterns of relating, and an established understanding of who we are (for better or worse) that frames our perceptions and how we interact with the world. To be fair, many times we are right, and this serves us well. Like when I experience hunger pangs in my body, I don't need to go through a whole exercise of "being curious" about what it means. I have lived long enough to know what hunger feels like, and I'm wise enough to know the best pathway forward is butter-frying a hot dog on the stove and chowing down on that bad boy.

But where true introspection is needed and would serve us well, we're sometimes afraid to look. Whether it's thinking the worst of yourself, or concern that you won't know how to fix whatever you may find broken, it can be easier to ignore it and continue existing as you were. You also may avoid getting curious with yourself because you *do* know what you will find, and the weight of it feels overwhelming. Financial anxieties and all the "shoulding" and "musting" about career, family life, housing, transportation, or investing can lead to feeling stuck, not knowing where to go next, and not wanting to engage with any of it. Not to mention if you've never seen good examples of what it's like to manage money well or save and spend with purpose.

This was the case for our friend Christine. Money was never talked about growing up, and credit cards were the only way she knew how to pay for stuff. By the time she graduated college, she not only had $38,000 in student loan debt but $14,000 of credit card debt on top of it. When she and her boyfriend started getting serious about marriage, she had a feeling of dread when they brought up finances. She had a decent job but still felt as though everything she wanted for her future was permanently out of reach. With her credit card and student loan debt still looming, she would get this sick, sinking feeling whenever she thought about how impossible buying a house or affording beautiful international trips felt. Things she thought she "should" do, things she saw her friends doing. Christine tried talking with her parents, but their philosophy with money was "It will all work out." Chatting with friends seemed wrong because some of them were in worse financial predicaments than her. Even her therapist was at a loss for what to do when her worries were disproportionate to her very "average" circumstances. With no real guidance, all Christine could do was ignore the issue. Unfortunately, disregarding what was happening and how she felt about it never got the debt paid, or removed the shame of spending, or even got her close to what she actually wanted to do with her money. Thankfully, Christine's story didn't end there. Eventually she was able to face the ever-growing gremlin of financial stress and anxiety with kind questions, curiosity about what she truly wanted, and smart steps toward those goals. This process made it possible for Christine to validate her anxiety, to see it as a warning light illuminating very real economic and individual concerns, while also coming up with a plan. The plan Christine made was connected to the things she found most important. She quickly discovered that she didn't care to buy a house anytime soon, so setting aside money for that goal was not important to her. And instead of Instagram-perfect resort experiences, she preferred camping in the woods. Once she cut out the things she didn't love, her money could go toward paying off credit card debt with room for the occasional takeout dinner and weekend trip. The more Christine learned about herself, the more she was able to tailor her spending and financial goals to what she truly wanted. And the more closely her plan reflected who she was, the more confident she felt about her finances.

Before we get to the type of curiosity that made these big shifts possible for Christine, we want to acknowledge the path to curiosity that's most common but often misguided: personality tests. The internet is full of gimmicks like: "Take this 5-min quiz to see what Disney princess you are," or "Look at these photos to determine if you're a bacon-wrapped shrimp or a pistachio-topped ice cream cone." (I made that last one up but can't say I wouldn't engage in that questionnaire!) I'm not throwing shade at these fun little quizzes, it's just that they don't actually help us in meaningful ways. It's recognizing our desire and need to know more about who we are but addressing it with fictional characters and personified food.

Beyond the trite quizzes, there are more in-depth personality tests like the Enneagram, Myers-Briggs, and DiSC. While these questionnaires are certainly more helpful than knowing if you're a bacon-wrapped shrimp, they won't provide the full picture needed to find what you value spending on. We are drawn to these tests because we ultimately want to understand ourselves, how we function, what makes us tick, how we are set apart from one another, and what makes us similar to others. What's more, we want to feel seen and understood. Ask anyone who has taken even just a short swim in the personality test pool and their eyes will light up with tales of their number or letter combination! Most can spend at least five minutes regaling us of the pros and cons of their unique internal makeup, what they enjoy and don't enjoy, how they do or don't mesh with their significant other, and the ways their personality impacts their breakfast order and which side of the bed they prefer sleeping on.

These assessments can be great tools, and I have seen them help many people take ownership of themselves, but they're just one part of the equation for orienting ourselves to a lifestyle we want. If we lean on them too heavily, we can overemphasize some aspects of who we are and underemphasize or omit others.

If curiosity is a large tent, personality tests are camping out inside that canvas. They are an excellent resource to utilize, but only a small section of the space. There's much more to explore inside the structure.

We also need to move past the noise of the self-help influencers and advertisements telling us that what we really need to aim at is perfect organization, or productivity, or minimalism, or sustainability, or wealth, or living an overwhelmingly nutritious/happy/thin/smiley/outdoorsy/adventurous life. Even if those adjectives do sound kinda great, we definitely don't need all of it, all the time. And we certainly don't need someone else telling us what we need.

Self-reflection is hard and messy, to the point where we may be tempted to skip it and go straight for the action part. This can include procrasti-spending. You know, avoiding the actual work by buying something that will help with the work. Like purchasing a self-reflection journal instead of just starting with one you already have. Or buying another self-help book instead of reading the ones already on your bookshelf.

It can be hard to pause and ask yourself if your spending lines up with what truly interests you, or if you've been influenced by what the internet, relationships, or even your horoscope tell you about yourself. Depending on your levels of connection with any one of these factors and how deeply rooted your patterns of behavior are, it can be hard to detangle "what's actually me" from "the fantasized, unrealistic version of me."

The type of curiosity-practicing we're advocating for is one that's kind and woven into our lives. This curiosity encompasses so much, including asking questions about ourselves, others, and the world around us. It also challenges our preconceived notions about any one of these categories. Curiosity re-evaluates and gives room for changing our minds or understanding something differently. It creates the space to decide you want to spend differently in different seasons. It provides permission to view debt differently, change your saving approach, modify your investing, and certainly opens the door to engage in perspectives about money that are different from yours without concern of it derailing you.

The barriers we face related to our own money stories and the tests we take to learn more about ourselves are not shortcomings. It's our own implementation and attachment of meaning that makes the difference in how these things impact our lifestyles and spending decisions. The solution? Not more tests, assessments, or information, but rather the formation of a habit of curiosity.

Getting Curious

There was a time in my life when I (Jill) was regularly feeling very exhausted. For me it wasn't the kind of exhaustion or tiredness where I just needed a nap, although I'm sure that would have helped. This was more of a deep weariness that sleep wasn't touching. I knew what I was experiencing had to do with the job I held as the director of a residential program for women exiting sexually exploitative circumstances. The hours I worked were long and the emotional toll was real, but that was the extent of my understanding. Everyday tasks were cumbersome, chitchat felt like a burden, I caught myself sighing *a lot*, and all I wanted to do was isolate. So I did. I told my husband I was too tired to see friends (something I usually enjoy) and opted instead for binge-watching TV or staying even later at work thinking, "If I get more done, it will free up time" (false!). Some nights I even read a book or took a long bath. The problem was—none of those things actually resolved the deeper issue. The truth was that I was burnt out and experiencing the effects of compassion fatigue. I needed to be paying attention to my needs and the indicator signs present so that I could better aim at well-being. Instead, I responded impulsively, doing things that may or may not have brought relief to me in the past, but things I was accustomed to doing, without considering whether they actually brought care and support into place.

It was during this season that my good friend and coworker Beth-ann presented me with a very simple and yet remarkably profound concept. She asked, "What's the deeper need present for you? Where are you feeling the most tired?" It was a nonjudgmental, non-leading question. She was being curious with me. I admit, I did not imme-diately know the answer, but as I thought about it, I recognized that the primary source of my exhaustion was relational. Due to the needs placed on me day-to-day and the conversational, problem-solving, compassion-focused, empathy efforts exerted, I was most depleted re-lationally. Working in a residential setting with clients very fresh in their recovery process and managing a team of employees, I was "on" nearly 24/7, and it was taking a toll on me. Of course, my friend's next question to me was "How can you care for yourself relationally?" It was a novel concept, and yet it made so much sense! Of course, I should respond to the need with something congruent with the need!

While I had been isolating, what I really needed was to spend time with trustworthy, caring friends where there was reciprocity in the rela-tionship (not just relational demands). This explained why the bubble baths and books weren't cutting it. They're good and all, but they were missing the mark in actually resolving the core issue.

So, I re-engaged in Sunday evening dinners with friends and had phone calls with loved ones during my long commutes. And while eventually there was a shelf-life to that job for me, I experienced symptom relief, perspective shifts, and a lightness inside myself as I responded to my needs in a way that matched the need.

All of this occurred because curiosity was modeled and encour-aged for me. When I lacked inquisitiveness and simply reacted, I did the exact opposite of what would help me. My "natural instinct" and social media's encouraged self-care efforts of isolation, TV-bingeing, and even bubble baths were not the right solution, and I would not have realized this if it weren't for slowing down and asking nonjudgmental, non-leading questions.

Since this experience, I have been on a journey of discovery. Like most journeys, it has included pit stops, wrong turns, and tantrums, but overall I am learning to ask myself questions. Before assumption and action, I am slowing down and reflecting on the situation, what's happening, and what this means about me and my response. If that's not Maslow's tippy-top triangle of self-actualization, I don't know what is!

Of course, this story of curiosity unearthing deeper needs and tangible solutions doesn't only apply to feeling burnt out at work but paints a picture of the power of being curious—with ourselves and others in all scenarios. Since this is something we can implement in every aspect of our personhood, including our spending, there are a few key steps I have found helpful in actually walking this out.

The first is to **create space**. We need to incorporate opportunities for pause if we want to have any level of insight into ourselves and the world around us. This could mean scheduling reflection times each night before bed, or it could look like creating margins within our day to process experiences as they happen. No matter the time of day or whether we write it down or simply think about it, intentionality and daily practice are necessary until this becomes a highly integrated part of our thought processes and how we move through our days.

Once we've created space, we need to **observe objectively**. This part entails some of that "scientific method" we all learned in fifth grade. Observe yourself as if you are a biologist in the wild looking on at some unknown creature, doing your best not to disturb it. We don't have judgments for this creature, there's no condemnation for what they're eating or how they're interacting with their species because all of it is information that will be useful to understanding how they operate. We are simply gathering data. We often avoid examining ourselves because we are our own worst critics. But it's not until we look at our actions without criticism that we are able to move on to the next step.

Inquiring inquisitively (can you tell we like alliteration?): This is the part where we ask questions. These questions come after our acceptance of objectivity and should be approached with care and kindness toward ourselves. We can ask:

What is happening in the environment around me?

How am I feeling?

What am I thinking?

How do I want to respond? What do I think that says about me?

What feels most important at this juncture?

What do my perceived "failures" tell me about myself?

These are some big questions. The type that can really help us see and accept more of ourselves and inform the steps we want to take with our spending. They are meant to engage us in a true discovery process.

You'll notice that none of them begin with "why." That's on purpose. It's not that "why" is a bad word, but often when it comes to curiosity, beginning with "why" can put us on the defense. It has a pretentious, condescending tone that can immediately cause our walls to go up, as we may feel judged by the question. It's the difference between "Why do you like shopping so much?" and "What is it about shopping that you most enjoy?" Do you see how they hit differently? One enlists automatic fight mode, and the other leads to "Hmm. Never thought about that, let me dig deeper!" When inquiring inquisitively, avoid the "why."

After we've answered some of these non-why questions, we **assess.** This is where we are now pairing information and facts with our thoughts and feelings and noticing any patterns that may exist. More questions at this stage can be helpful as we synthesize and begin to pull everything together.

What do the various data points mean?

What do I make of my feelings and my conscious or subconscious responses?

Are there any patterns of behavior or thoughts that I'm noticing?

What am I learning about myself?

How do I function best?

Now it's time to **respond**. At this stage we now have the opportunity for informed action, which is quite different from uninformed, unintentional reactivity. Given what we've learned about ourselves, we can utilize that knowledge in a way that is kind and provides space for next steps. This action feels different from "shoulding" and "musting" on ourselves. This step acknowledges the realities of circumstances, how you may have responded in the past, and gives room to trailblaze new paths where needed. Or it may lead you to continue on in the way you were going with more confidence!

And once we've done all that, we do it again! **Repeat** the process, because inevitably there will be an opportunity for these steps again today, tomorrow, and in the weeks/months/years to come! The good news is, this process becomes less and less cumbersome and time-consuming the more you do it and will eventually become second nature. As you implement these practices, you will notice that curiosity doesn't just lead to learning more about what you love, it also builds the skills of creativity, problem solving, research, and more. All skills that are essential to practicing values-based spending. You can even turn around and give the gift of curiosity to others by asking open-ended questions that aim at valuing and understanding.

Engaging in these steps of **creating space**, **observing objectively**, **inquiring inquisitively**, **assessing**, and **responding** will almost certainly train us in the way of a growth mindset. One that is not fixed but gives way to refinement, experiencing the fruit of our efforts, and more realized potential inside ourselves. It will also help us move away from the all-or-nothing, catastrophizing, overgeneralizing ways of thinking and live more in the reality of the present as we give ourselves space to think more critically in a nonjudgmental manner. Not that we still won't be drawn to these unhelpful thinking patterns, but we can catch ourselves and gently move to a place of better thinking. Which inevitably leads to better, more informed actions.

I went through these steps of curiosity when my husband, Eric, and I were hit with an unexpected hefty tax bill. In addition to needing to fork over money that I had not previously planned to give to Uncle Sam, I was also navigating feelings of shame, failure, embarrassment, and frustration. "I'm the cohost of a personal finance podcast, how did I not see this coming? How did I not plan for this? How do I make sure *nobody* finds out about this?" I questioned myself, my abilities, even my fit-ness for talking about money to a large audience when I'm sitting in my accountant's office with a lump in my throat trying to do ninja-math, meanwhile recognizing that another unexpected bill could mean financial ruin.

I was catastrophizing, immediately going to the worst-case scenario in my head. I even set a rule for Eric and me that we couldn't ride our scooters for the next month because, in my mind, if we got in an accident that would mean a large medical bill that could potentially bankrupt us. I am laughing now as I write this, but the circumstances at the time truly felt dire to me. Of course I was forgetting about the emergency fund we still had, the insurance (albeit sucky) that would help offset costs of medical needs, and don't forget all my knowledge of negotiating, saving, and spending better (thanks to Jen and my Frugal Friends community)! None of that mattered in the face of failure. Yet as I **created space** to take some deep breaths, spoke to a few trusted friends, and was challenged to bring some contrasting thoughts and facts to the situation, I was able to **observe objectively** and **inquire inquisitively**. My healthier, more curious, inner monologue went something like this: "What led me to think that this year I did not need to set a percentage aside for taxes?" Notice the non-why question!

Turns out it is a very common mistake (even according to tax experts) for people with multiple W2s to not select extra withholding when needed. As I **assessed** both the facts and my emotions about it all, I realized that this was our first year ever not working as independent contractors in some capacity, and I was experiencing the reality of my illiteracy in this new tax terrain. Now I know. Now I can **respond** by course correcting for next time and turn around and inform others so they don't have to experience the same thing. Hey, I'm starting to feel more in control and empowered in my situation. I'm not feeling as embarrassed. Maybe I will write about this in my book (lol).

It was from this place that I could then rework my catastrophizing and overgeneralizing inner thoughts and outward decisions. I found myself grateful that we did have the money to cover the expense. It was a lot, and it took us time to recover, but we were in a much different place than five years prior. It didn't ruin us. I was glad for a helpful accountant who didn't shame us but instead assisted us (and kept us out of tax prison . . . that's a thing, right?). I was glad for a community I could make mistakes in front of, a group of friends who had my back (including our readers and listeners!) who modeled grace and were full of encouragement on this journey where none of us are doing it perfectly!

And suddenly I wasn't trapped in my situation. I was moving forward with full awareness of my reality, a plan of attack in place, and thoughts that weren't debilitating. Curiosity helped me to manage myself in the midst of something really stressful and overwhelming and make important shifts where needed.

It was in this place of action that I felt the most relief within my circumstances. We were able to make the decision to cut back on eating out, a discretionary spending area where Eric and I are prone to indulge. Instead, we cooked at home more and put that money toward "replenishing the coffers," as I called it. I felt good about this course correction and our ability to change the trajectory of our situation. We also adjusted our tax withholdings so we would not find ourselves in this place again.

The freedom and control I was able to find over a stressful financial situation felt empowering. Curiosity helped me to be kind to myself and find real solutions.

How Do I Integrate All of This?

A habit of curiosity is the foundation to knowing what you love and value. Your spending will evolve as you get to know yourself better. Something you think you love now can be something you learn you only loved one part of, and you can start to invest in that part without wasting money on the part you don't care about as much.

Asking ourselves better, less judgy questions will help us accurately discover what we like, what brings us joy, the lifestyle we are most enthused about, and the person we want to become. This type of refinement brings clarity to nearly every decision we will make regarding our personal lives. As we ask:

What is it about me that is drawn to this thing?

What about my experiences, upbringing, or personality causes me to find myself in this pattern?

What am I most proud of?

What brings me the most joy?

These discoveries, born out of curiosity, don't just impact spending, investing, and saving, but can also influence our careers and life trajectories. When we refine and grow our identity as an employee, subcontractor, freelancer, or entrepreneur, we can find ourselves in roles that are more suited for us. This can lead to increased enjoyment, expression of self, and contentment. And dare I say, possibly more money? Granted, your job doesn't have to be your passion, but it can align with your values, and that's a beautiful thing.

You are likely to meet your values most accurately when you have a fuller understanding of who you are and what makes you tick. It's what can lead to sustainability and longevity far beyond a prescribed set of rules or "shoulds" and "musts" imposed on you by financial gurus or society at large. When you've put in the work and are making decisions around what actually matters to you, not what others have told you should matter, you get to make the rules!

The actions you take with your money based on your curiosity will allow you to see you don't actually love everything. You like a lot of things, you love some things, and not all of it actually requires you to spend. The adjustments you make as a result will sometimes be small shifts in mindset, sometimes they'll be big one-time decisions, and other times they will be minor, nuanced tweaks. Knowing what can be changed or modified relies upon your knowledge of what's going on, and the best way to do this is by looking. We will walk you through how to do this in the next chapter.

⚡ Lightning Round ⚡

What is a recent financial flub you've been embarrassed about?

⚠ Action Step

With your lightning round answer, take yourself through the steps of curiosity: create space, observe objectively, inquire inquisitively, assess, and respond.

CHAPTER 3

Can't Buy Me Love

As a birthday gift for my mother-in-law one year, Eric and I (Jill) attempted to digitize old family VHS videos. We didn't get too far with this. It's a long process. But we did get to enjoy one particular scene from Christmas morning 1992 when the whole family got a computer. It was Eric's older brothers who got to unwrap the computer and desktop screen. It was a big gift, and they were over the moon excited. Then the camera cuts to four-year-old Eric unwrapping his gift, only to reveal a power strip. Trying not to show disappointment, he shouted "A PLUG!" Seeing what his brothers got, I can only imagine what his little brain was thinking when he received an extension cord. But he played it cool and tried to make it seem like it was what he always wanted. We laughed so hard watching it all unfold.

Rest assured Eric got to play his fair share of Math Blaster on the new computer. But it got me thinking that his Christmas morning experience is often how life can feel. When everyone around us seems to be acquiring big, new, cool gadgets and all we can afford is a power strip, it's hard to hide our disappointment. People say money doesn't buy love, happiness, or joy, but most of us would rather be sad in a Range Rover than a rusting car. We need money to support the things we love, even if luxury vehicles will never be something we buy.

So, what happens when you have "computer" values but only "plug" money? When you're finding it hard to afford what you love, there are many solutions, the most obvious being to make more money.

While we do encourage earning more, that method can take time. On the other hand, the quickest way to free up income is by decreasing expenses. We frugal people do love this option.

But there is a third option. A radical middle option, if you will. One where we can keep both our income and spending amounts the same (assuming we're not outspending what we earn) and just shift what we're spending on. Take out the impulse and mindless purchases and replace them with more values-aligned purchases. This could mean ordering takeout less and more weekend getaways, or fewer subscriptions and more retirement investing, or no new upgrades and more debt freedom. Essentially, we're fleshing out values-based spending.

While the first two methods for freeing up money focus on numbers, values-based spending focuses on purchasing decisions and the needs behind them. Earning more and buying less looks at *how much* we purchase, whereas values-based spending looks at *what* we purchase. In the real world, we do need all three: earning more, buying less, and making mindful spending decisions. One is not more important than the others—they're all important in varying measures, in different seasons. But because so many other books focus on the numbers, we're going to keep focusing on the purchases and the ways our shifts in this third category also help us get the things we really want.

We didn't start with the math, or by making budgets (although we *will* get to that). Not because those things aren't important, but because so often when we try to take action without having a strong mental foundation backing up that action, it inevitably doesn't go as planned. And we can feel like the failure. But the failure isn't you, it's the order in which money concerns are tackled that's to blame. The reason starting with a budget or simply slicing up your credit cards isn't a long-term solution to a spending problem is because they aren't tethered to anything. Budgets manage the "how much" and beginning with math problems ignores the context of the equation. When we don't understand what's going on behind the numbers on the credit card statements, we're less likely to value them. Because we rarely value what we don't understand. It's why taking time to practice curiosity and learn what you value is so important. It's also why you need to start by understanding your past actions before diving into future action.

With clear eyes, awareness of what you care about, non-shaming questions of curiosity, and permission to not get it perfect, you're ready to take the next step of looking at your current spending.

The Glorious 90-Day Transaction Inventory

When people are interested in changing their spending habits, they will ask where to start. We always say if you want to make changes to what you will buy, you need to figure out what you're currently buying! The first tangible step to do this is to begin with a 90-day transaction inventory. This inventory involves pulling all your transactions from the last ninety days, pasting them all into a spreadsheet, and reviewing it thoroughly (don't worry, we'll explain what to look for). Your inventory will include everything from your bills and subscriptions to your discretionary spending as well as irregular and one-time purchases. You'll gather it all digitally by downloading a .csv file from your bank or budgeting app or copying and pasting your transactions into a spreadsheet. Alternatively, if you love printing things out, then gather all your highlighters, colored pens, and sticky notes and do you!

The reason we say ninety days is because month to month, things change. Every month brings new, often unexpected, expenses. From birthday parties and weddings to unexpected or irregular bills, no month looks the same as the previous months. But while every month is different, they're not that different. So, a three-month inventory can give you a clear picture of where your money is going most frequently. Will this exercise capture everything? No. Will it be close enough? Absolutely.

Once you've got that list of transactions, you can clean it up so it's easier to navigate. All you really need is *when* the purchase was made, *where* the purchase was made, and *how much* it cost. We have a free 90-day transaction inventory spreadsheet template and video walkthrough of how to do one in the resources page for this book at frugalfriendspodcast.com/book.

Now that you have every transaction in one place, sort them by date. Arranging them this way allows you to look at your expenses in relation to time, which can reveal patterns and other clues about how you spend. Remember, you are reviewing these transactions with curiosity, not criticism. Next to each transaction, log what you remember as the purpose behind it. You can ask yourself things like:

Who was I with before, during, or after I made the purchase?

Where was I coming from or on my way to when I made the purchase?

What was going on or what was I doing right before I bought this?

How was I feeling before or after I made this purchase?

Was I trying to fulfill a value by making this purchase?

Did it give me the result that I wanted?

You don't have to answer all those questions for every purchase; they're just examples to jog your memory. This is an unbiased exercise in learning more about what causes you to spend money. By exploring each expense, you start to see which purchases could most easily be eliminated, which ones are currently aligned with your values, and if there are any environmental changes you can make to avoid some spending. You also learn more about who you are and why you spend what you spend, which will ultimately lead to greater understanding of your values.

Don't expect to be able to do this all in an hour or try to rush through it. Give the glorious 90-day transaction inventory the time it deserves. But don't overthink it either. If the idea of a transaction inventory feels overwhelming, try tackling a month at a time and finish it over three days. Don't feel embarrassed or like you're not normal if this takes you longer to complete than you thought it would. This isn't a test, there are no right answers, and you are not required to submit a response for every transaction. But—spoiler alert—we'll be referencing it a lot moving forward, so it is important to try.

Muffin Moment

You might look at your transaction inventory and think, "I love too much, I just need to earn more." Again, income is important. We don't want to minimize the significance of earning an amount of money that meets both your needs and your desires. But if you don't know *how* to spend it, earning more of it won't solve your problems or get you closer to the things you love. It may even create more problems, like it did for our friends Haley and Justin. At twenty-four years old, after his grandma died of mesothelioma, Justin received a $600,000 wrongful death lawsuit payout. Haley and Justin both grew up in lower-income single-mom households in California. Households where, when you have extra money, you spend it because you don't know when you're going to get it again.

Initially, they did practical things with it. Justin paid off his undergrad student loans, bought himself a nice used car, and even paid off the remaining balance on his mom's vehicle. But after that, with no clear direction on what to do with that much money, the inevitable happened. It got spent.

Haley remembers vividly when the shift took place. She recalled, "We went to the Melting Pot with his siblings because they also received the same amount of money. And we dropped $600 on dinner between all of us. At the Melting Pot."

They were dining out, taking vacations, and purchasing a new house with new furnishings to fill it. They weren't buying Lambos and Gucci, but they were experiencing lifestyle inflation on an accelerated timeline.

Less than four years later, not only was all $600,000 gone, but they had racked up an additional $220,000 of debt. They both enrolled in grad school at a private university, bought a timeshare, financed an SUV for their growing family, and started using credit cards because someone told them you needed credit card debt to have a good credit score. And instead of paying for everything, they thought the safe thing to do was to hold on to the cash and make low monthly payments on the big stuff. Except they didn't hold on to the cash.

In September 2019, the two teachers were finally on a salary system, making the most money they'd ever made and getting paid consistently on the first of every month. This particular month, they took a trip for their one-year anniversary, and by the time they returned on the 8th, they had no money left in their bank account. All their money for the whole month was already spent, and they had to rely on credit cards until their next payday. That was the moment they realized something had to change. But nothing changed—yet. A couple of weeks later, Haley went to Costco and came back with two-for-$7 pumpkin muffins. A delicious treat that Justin should have thanked her for. Instead, it led to an argument that, at its core, was about not having an extra $7 for muffins.

"That was the turning point," Haley said, "where we decided this isn't working. If we're making the most money we've ever made, relying on credit cards, and we don't have $7 for muffins, this is a big problem, and we have to change it."

If you're here reading this book today, it may be because you've had your own muffin moment, or maybe you see it on the horizon and you're trying to avoid it. Time and time again we have the illusion that more money will solve our spending problems, but we know from experience and from countless stories like Haley and Justin's that more money only gives more fuel to spending fires.

Your income is your greatest tool for getting the things you need and want from life, but we live in a world that is intentionally designed to compel you to spend it. From childhood hardships to well-crafted advertising, without the knowledge of how to spend money well, we will continue to spend again and again on things that don't get us what we truly want. Wherever you're at right now, whether you're trying to increase your income, optimize it, or free yourself from the need for so much of it, values-based spending can help. It's what will allow you to make better spending decisions with your money now, and it's also what will prepare you for when you do earn more in the future!

But our spending is always going to be limited to the income we have at the given moment. So now the question becomes: How do we afford the things we love without unlimited income?

What Matters Most

Our friend Allison grappled with this question. She and her husband, Matt, had over $111,000 of debt living on two teachers' salaries. She thought she was doing well with money. She knew how much money was coming in every month and would spend all the way down to zero. "My ultimate goal was to not overdraft, and I was really good at it. I thought that as long as I wasn't going into the negatives, that I was great."

Until she got pregnant.

She realized they couldn't afford childcare or for her to stay home with their baby. Much less the medical bills, diapers, and every other expense that would come up. Like most of us, Allison couldn't afford everything. Without an unlimited income, she couldn't afford daycare, debt, and all the impulse purchases at the same time. So, she prioritized. She saw that the quickest way to free up income for daycare was paying off debt, so they made that their number one priority.

But there was no switch to flip to turn off the dopamine hits of shopping. Allison struggled with feelings of anger for getting into debt, resentment of her budget, and guilt for still wanting to "spend to zero" with a baby on the way. But she stuck with it. And after four or five months, she felt a shift.

"In the beginning, I valued everything because that's what the world told me to do. But I truly didn't understand what I valued spending money on. It took me not spending money for a time, and then slowly introducing those things back into my spending, for me to see what I value." It wasn't easy, but that season began to show her the things she didn't value so she could spend without guilt on the things she did value. Allison and Matt paid off their six-figure debt in less than five years. Along the way she realized she didn't value the "deals" at the store as much as she thought. Instead, she wanted to travel. While they did do some traveling while paying off debt, it was minimal. Now that they're debt-free and her kids are out of daycare, they take amazing camping trips to national parks and even surprise trips to Disney! But the freedom to spend on that only came after a season in which they prioritized paying off debt.

Prioritization is simply defining what matters most and tackling those things in sequence. It's the key to buying what we want on a limited income and it's what helps us recognize that if everything is important, nothing is important. This is where we start to define how to afford the things we love, especially the physical things, and the financial goals we need to pursue to get more of the things we value that money can't buy. Prioritization doesn't make any one need or goal less worthwhile. It simply conserves our limited resources, tangible and intangible, to give us the best and fullest life possible in every season. It's what helps us to say no to things that don't matter and yes to things that do.

So how do we define what matters most?

First, we need to think about those four F's and what we want from each of those areas: with our family and friends, in our faith communities, and fulfilling work. For Allison, she obviously valued her new baby! But she also loved her work as a teacher and didn't want to leave. They decided paying off their debt faster would be the best way to free up more income for the future.

When we think about making financial goals, we live by this principle: *What's one thing I can do now that will get me more of what I value in the future?* There's no shortage of good financial goals out there, but with a limited income, we need to focus on one at a time. And if you're only going to focus on one at a time, choose the one with the biggest impact. Often this means paying off debt, but it doesn't have to be. It could also be saving for an event, like a wedding or birth of a baby, or investing for retirement. Everyone's financial goal will look different. Choose the one that gets you closer to what you love.

Once you've defined the financial goals that matter most, you can move on to the tangible things you like to buy. To define the things you value most in this category, it can actually be helpful to start with what matters least. Go back through your 90-day transaction inventory and identify the purchases that didn't fulfill the need you wanted or make you feel the way you intended. Look for subscriptions you don't use or didn't realize you had and purchases you don't remember making. These are good indicators that those purchases are not things you love. Some other questions you can ask about your purchases that can help you identify things that don't matter are:

Did I feel pressured to buy or contribute to this?

Was the act of purchasing more important than the purchase itself?

Was the purchase influenced by some unattainable standard, or something seen on social media?

With physical pen and paper, make a list, a commitment rather, of five to ten things you decide you no longer value, and as a result will no longer spend on for the foreseeable future. Your list should be short, realistic, and simple to follow through on. The list should not include your mortgage or rent payment—please keep a roof over your head. That said, you may find that your list gives you inspiration to be creative with expenses that seem difficult to change. For example, maybe you find you don't want to be a homeowner anymore, but selling isn't the best decision for you right now. Simply identifying what you don't value could lead you on the path to rent your home out and go rent somewhere else you truly want to be. This example may feel extreme, but we want to show you that when you start getting curious, specifically about what you've assumed is set in stone, you can start to ask questions and come up with creative options to spend in greater alignment with what you value.

Next, you can start to explore the things you do value. Go through your 90-day transaction inventory and look for the things you bought that you loved and still love three months later. Things that fully met an internal need or, if you're a Marie Kondo fan, sparked joy for you. Make note of all of them, no matter how many of them there are. You might be surprised to find that they're fewer and farther between than you would've thought. And you may start to see a strange phenomena in which you can have transactions that are both aligned and out of alignment with your values within a single expense category.

For example, coffee.

One coffee could be aligned with your values because it gave you time with a friend or a place to study that was out of the chaos of your home. Another coffee could just have been a habit purchase. You look at your list and realize that whenever you go to the store, you pick up a drink there or on the way. You don't know why, you barely remember it, it's just a thing you always do. The same purchase, made for different reasons, was both something you loved and something you didn't. That's why it's important to make a note of what triggered each of your purchases on that initial overview of your inventory.

As you're understanding more about your habits and spending behaviors, you can make intentional spending decisions that don't cut out an entire category, just the transactions that are mindless and don't get you what you love. Coffee isn't the enemy. The location is not the enemy. Ultimately, we want your goal to be to know what you're buying and the reason you're buying it.

There is no perfect list of values-aligned expenses and no perfect order to arrange them in. But you can make a pretty good one by writing down the things you've identified you value buying and then ordering them from what matters most to what matters less. Everything on your list will matter, but the things at the top of the list will matter most.

Cutting out things you are used to buying or only buying the things at the tippy-top of your "what matters most list" will be hard. Even though you did the work of prioritizing and named the things you want to say no to for now, it will still be difficult to interrupt deeply ingrained patterns. This is why we say values-based spending requires sacrifice, but it's not deprivation. You may feel sad about saying no to things you once said yes to without thinking, but prioritizing makes sure you're always getting the things that you love most, so it's not complete destitution.

When I (Jill) went through this process, it meant prioritizing paying cash for our house renovations for two years. After that, I shifted my focus to invest more heavily in our retirement accounts. For my friend Rachel, she's choosing to reside in an affordable cost of living area so she can consistently max out her retirement investments and still travel multiple times a year. Another friend, Cindy, is prioritizing paying off her house early, which is made possible by putting a new car purchase, home upgrades, and expensive trips on the back burner.

We know it seems like a long list of priorities to fit into a short income, but you don't have to be doing the most all the time. The things that are of highest importance to you may shift and your capacity to pursue what you value will also change. Making spending decisions that reflect this knowledge is what we call embracing your season.

Embracing Your Season

An important detail in how Allison prioritized her spending was her specific season of life. She knew that the one decision she could make now that would get her more of what she loved in the future was paying off debt. She also knew that having a baby was not cheap, but that what she would spend on after giving birth is different from what she would spend on when the kids are grown. These ebbs and flows of life are what informed her on how to make the most of her current reality.

Just like Allison, what your money can do is inextricably linked to your current reality, your season of life. It's your season that defines your circumstances and dictates a good amount of your financial behaviors.

Whether single, married, divorced, with kids or without kids, a homeowner or renter, it all impacts the spending decisions you make. A married homeowner with children has different responsibilities and demands on their money from a single childless person who rents. And both need to make financial decisions in light of their season. You also may experience short and long seasons, seasons related to external circumstances, and others resulting from internal realities; there are good and welcomed seasons and there are not-so-great, unwelcomed seasons. All of it matters.

While there are times that your present circumstances may feel like a hindrance to the life you desire, we're taking the perspective that choosing to embrace, honor, and work within your season is fundamental to navigating the journey with purpose.

Bringing your spending into alignment with your season and your values means identifying and accepting what makes sense for *you* in this timing, where you've come from, and where you want to be going. Because it's not just about this current season, it's also about the future. It's important to value and put resources toward the seasons to come both near and distant. Whether that means planning and preparing for a fun vacation or getting your finances to a good place in order to move, retire well, or pay for your child's college. All of it will require prioritization and embracing the limitations of your season while also allowing yourself to be the dynamic, flexible, innovative renegade you are!

But we also understand the flip side. Your season may not make you feel like a renegade. Instead it might make you feel just plain 'ol tired. Sometimes previous seasons, experiences, and mindsets around money can keep you from seeing what's possible in your current season.

Whether unfortunate events happened, or you chose a challenging path, life can be really crummy. We acknowledge that even though we have control over some things, we don't have control over all things! And regardless of whether the cause was our choice, other people's choices, or natural occurrences, there can be a corresponding emotional impact.

This can create obstacles for moving forward, future thinking and planning, or identifying hope. If you find yourself living in a perpetual state of stress, anxiety, and exhaustion, it can lead to difficulties in making wise financial decisions, or even identifying what you want your life to look like.

This book is not about exiting the stress response cycle or effectively treating anxiety, but it is worth noting these factors play into tough seasons and may help you understand why life doesn't and can't always look the way influencers attempt to portray it. Having knowledge of and naming our current obstacles and difficulties is what allows us to understand, value, and live as best as possible *within* the circumstances.

Your "radical middle," the version of life that allows you to find and spend on the things you value while also recognizing and rejecting the things that don't, will come with parameters. Our seasons rarely allow us to do and buy all the things we want, but it's here that we can allow our creativity to flourish.

In research conducted by the *Harvard Business Review*, it was found that in a variety of settings, teams of people functioned best when given reasonable constraints for a project. Those with parameters like a budget, a set timeline, and rationed resources, showed high levels of motivation, creativity, and ability to connect information and bring about innovative solutions. Alternatively, when people were given no constraints on budget or time, the output revealed very little ingenuity or effort.

The same is true for you! Parameters, limitations, and constraints provide the context to create. Your income, family, education level, and living situation don't need to be viewed as hindrances to the way you want to spend. Instead, they can be the things that inform *how* you spend. They are the guidelines for your creativity and help to define how you can have the things you love within the realities of your situation. And even the things you want to change in order to have more of what you love.

For me (Jill), in my debt payoff endeavor, I often felt frustrated by the limitations of my season. Being new in my career, saddled with student loan debt, and only making a meager salary had me wishing I could skip ahead a few years to when I imagined things would be better. Ultimately, it took me and my husband, Eric, seven years to pay off $60,000 of debt. Those numbers are not remarkable. That time-to-money ratio isn't newsworthy. *But* over the course of those seven years, we did become debt free! In a time when our annual household income fluctuated between $45,000 and $60,000, we couldn't be the people who paid everything off in a matter of months. While our story will never be the title of some clickbait-y article, we still ended it debt-free.

In the very beginning of paying down our debt, I had hopes of getting rid of all of it in five years. But as time went on, I realized it was going to take a bit longer. It didn't feel great, but recognizing our limitations and the realities of our season allowed us to embrace a new, extended timeline for debt payoff. So much happened in those years. Eric changed careers, I switched jobs (a few times), we moved nearly every year, and I got my master's degree. Some of those circumstances gave us an opportunity to throw chunks of money toward our debt, and at other times we needed to reel it in and simply focus on covering our living expenses.

While there were certainly disappointments and moments of impatience throughout the journey, I can say without doubt that I have no regrets. As I look back now, I don't wish that we had broken our backs to pay it off quicker. Life was lived in those seven years, and little by little the debt dwindled. It's what those seasons of life allowed for, and working within my reality, rather than against it, made all the difference for me. It didn't just impact my ability to accomplish a long-term goal, it also shifted the way I viewed myself. I went from feeling like a dummy for all the student loan debt I took out to embracing what was possible for me and the things I was accomplishing in the midst of slowly paying off the loans.

Working within our limitations is what allowed Eric and me to choose creative living situations, like house-sitting in a log cabin for a year and full-time RV-ing for two years. Those choices afforded us what we love, as we prioritized job flexibility and investing in my graduate education. We found ways to get the things we wanted despite what felt like hindrances at the time.

As you think about your own circumstances, it's possible that reframing your thoughts about your season will open up possibilities in the way you live and spend. Are there creative decisions you can make that will allow you to meet your money goals? How can your current "limitations" inform your spending and next steps?

Even if you're stepping out of a difficult season or financial hurdles, the beautiful thing about healing and change is that it happens *as you are going*.

You may need to take it easy at times, but it doesn't mean stagnation. New experiences, forward progress, and trusted people all offer great opportunities to shift spending habits and uncover capabilities above and beyond what you may have thought possible.

I, for one, never would have thought nontraditional housing would be what helped me pay off debt, but limitations brought to the surface new ideas. These experiences forever shaped me and played a part in who I am becoming.

You too are in your process of becoming, and your season is what's shaping that, not hindering it. So, while your current season may not afford you *everything* you love, embracing it and prioritizing your values is how you get what matters most.

And that's a wrap on part 1. Hopefully by now you have a solid grasp on how you define "what you love" and know what the journey looks like to find and buy those things. You also know that buying what you love doesn't mean spending your whole paycheck on all the restaurant appetizers, nor is it all going to fulfill your deepest needs for quality time. It's somewhere in the radical middle of them. And to find that radical middle, you have to build a habit of curiosity. Curiosity that seeks to understand without judgment. And know that the road to pursuing the things you love won't be paved. You'll have to navigate your income, season, and values, which may include delayed gratification at times, but ultimately none of it should feel like deprivation. You're laying down some things so you can pick up the more important things. Whether that be for now or in the future.

In the next section we'll navigate the noes. Why it's so hard to say no, how to say better no's, and how to navigate places where you can say no, but not fully. All in the hopes of helping you journey through the nuances of values-based spending.

⚡ Lightning Round ⚡

What expenses are most important to you in your current season, and how are you prioritizing them?

⚠

Action Step

Complete the 90-day transaction inventory. Go through your transactions and try to note the reason behind each one. Remember, we have a full video walkthrough of the 90-day transaction inventory process at frugalfriends podcast.com/book.

PART 2

Say No to What You Don't

CHAPTER 4

Manufactured Desire

There's someone you've probably never heard of but who impacts every day of your life and is directly responsible for many of the dollars you've spent: Edward Bernays.

Bernays is known as the father of public relations and was named one of the hundred most influential Americans of the twentieth century. He wrote several works that laid the foundation for how companies promote themselves today.

In 1927, Bernays started working for the American Tobacco Company with an objective to increase cigarette sales among women. His first strategy? To persuade women to smoke cigarettes instead of eating. Bernays began by promoting the ideal of thinness itself, using photographers, artists, newspapers, and magazines to promote the "special beauty" of thin women. He then found medical authorities to advocate for the choice of cigarettes over sweets. It worked. Women started smoking. But there was still a taboo about women smoking in public. Women had just gained the right to vote in 1920, prompting Bernays to exploit the emboldened suffrage movement by turning cigarettes into a symbol of rebellion and equal rights. Bernays started the movement by hiring women to march in the 1929 NYC Easter Sunday Parade while smoking their "torches of freedom."

That's not the most important thing we want you to know about him. We're just setting the tone so you can form an appropriate opinion of him.

His biggest impact on your wallet comes from his 1928 best-selling book, *Propaganda*. The book explored the psychology behind manipulating the masses and how to "engineer consent" for political gain. Bernays got his passion for psychology from his uncle Sigmund Freud. Yeah, that Freud.

Bernays made a career of intentionally tapping in to people's irrationality and unconscious impulses to sell products. He believed that our unconscious "animal instincts" could be used to sell middle-class consumers products they didn't strictly need, a practice that was previously reserved for the uber wealthy. He marketed products not to meet a need, but to reflect the buyer's personal identity. Sound familiar?

It's not like the desire for things is new, but before mass production, you had to wait for them. Things were made by hand, they took time, and cost a higher percentage of your household income. By the end of the Industrial Revolution in 1840, goods were much easier to manufacture. But in order for these large-scale productions to keep up with costs, the market had to inform people that they no longer had to wait or pay as much to get what they want when they want it. My favorite quote from *Propaganda* sums up Bernays's marketing framework for profitable mass production:

"Mass production is profitable only if its rhythm can be maintained—that is, if it can continue to sell its product in steady or increasing quantity. . . . Today supply must actively seek to create its corresponding demand . . . [and] cannot afford to wait until the public asks for its product; it must maintain constant touch, through advertising and propaganda . . . to assure itself the continuous demand which alone will make its costly plant profitable."

Companies are not just in the business of manufacturing products; they're also in the business of manufacturing desire.

Constantly Moving Happiness Machines

Bernays was also instrumental in creating the idea that recreational shopping is a civic duty. President Herbert Hoover was one of several politicians who sought out Bernays to help sell his policy ideas and campaigns. Hoover once told a group of advertising executives: "You have taken over the job of creating desire and have transformed people into constantly moving happiness machines, machines which have become the key to economic progress."

Bernays was a mastermind, but he wasn't alone in creating the consumer culture we see today. Edward Cowdrick, an economist, penned "the new economic gospel of consumption," promoting the idea that blue-collar families could be educated in the new "skills of consumption." And Charles Kettering, Director of Research at General Motors from 1920–1947, is said to have told his team to "[Pursue] constant improvement and change so that the customer will be stimulated to desire the new product enough to buy it to replace the one he has."

Over the last one hundred years, capitalism has preserved rapid growth for its shareholders by taking away our identities as people and turning us into consumers. Consumers with an unquenchable thirst for more. And it worked. The U.S. Bureau of Labor Statistics reported that in 1901 families spent an average of 20 percent of their income on "non-necessities." A century later, in 2002, that figure was 50 percent. *Chicago Tribune* journalist Mary T. Schmich coined the term "retail therapy" in 1986 when she wrote, "We've become a nation measuring out our lives in shopping bags and nursing our psychic ills through retail therapy."

We think it's important to understand the history of consumerism in America not because we're anti-capitalism or because we want you to be angry about this systemic deception. But to remind you that many of your desires do not come from within. There are people in offices whose job it is to manipulate our good-intentioned desires and our insecurities to turn us into machines that are constantly seeking happiness. Marketing and advertising have conditioned us from birth to be dissatisfied with what we have and where we've been and believe the next new thing or place will be the solution. And it's led to a change in the chemical activity in our brains that makes it ever more appealing to spend.

Trained Monkeys

In her book *Dopamine Nation*, psychiatrist Dr. Anna Lembke recounts stories from her decades of treating patients for addiction. She's seen every kind of addiction, from the common to the NSFW (not safe for work). She even recounts her own short-lived addiction to romance novels, a high we've personally experienced once or twice . . . or more. The common thread she cites among all addictions is the release of dopamine.

Dopamine is the chemical messenger in your brain that creates a good feeling when you do something enjoyable. It also impacts memory and motivation, making you want to repeat whatever got you that good feeling, which is why dopamine plays a role in addiction. Many things trigger dopamine release: your favorite activities, scrolling social media, sugar, sex, shopping, and, of course, certain drugs. Scientists now believe that dopamine's role isn't to directly cause good feelings, but to serve as a reinforcement for remembering and repeating pleasurable experiences. So, in the case of drug addiction, surges in dopamine don't stop at causing euphoria, they teach your brain, in unnaturally heightened amounts, to remember the experience. So, while anything that triggers dopamine release can be addictive, it's far easier to change dopamine-induced habits in things that don't elicit as much dopamine, like shopping. But just because it's doable doesn't mean it's easy.

Every time you check out at a store or hit the Buy Now button, dopamine is released and you have a pleasurable experience, but we know that experience doesn't last. So why do we keep pleasure shopping? Because dopamine is simultaneously teaching your brain to remember the pleasurable experience of every purchase, no matter how short-lived. And the more purchases you have, the more pleasurable experiences you have to draw from. It doesn't stop there, because every time you remember that pleasurable experience, more dopamine is released, further instilling in your brain that shopping = fun and happiness.

Even when we know an action is ultimately bad for us, dopamine inundates us with reminders of how sweet the instant gratification is. It's why we eat more than we want, scroll late into the night, and shop beyond what we can reasonably afford. It doesn't matter how many times someone tells us we need to save for retirement or that buying all this new stuff is contributing to 60 percent of all greenhouse gas emissions, the instant gratification is all that matters.

Neuroscientist Robert Sapolsky trained monkeys to know that if they pressed a button ten times, after a signal lit up, then on the tenth button press, a food treat would appear. During each signal, work, reward cycle, Sapolsky measured the amount and timing of dopamine release in the monkeys' brains. You might predict that dopamine release would spike with the reward, but in reality the opposite was true. The dopamine release started as soon as the signal lit up, peaked up until the ninth press, and plummeted immediately after the tenth pressing. Instead of dopamine being released when the brain received a reward, it was released in anticipation of one.

Our desires may be manufactured, but our dopamine is real. And most of the dopamine released in our shopping isn't in getting the things, it's in the act of shopping. A fact that hasn't gone unnoticed by financial technology companies. If marketers are focused on your desires and insecurities, fintech companies are manufacturing the experience of shopping. They are always looking for ways to make the experience of shopping more "frictionless."

I (Jen) was scrolling Instagram recently and saw an ad for an adult paint-by-numbers kit. Now, I am a horrible artist and get very frustrated by how bad I am. But in that moment, I wanted what that girl in the picture had! That relaxing experience and a piece of art to show for it! I just knew it would be better than the freehand forest I painted at that sip and paint five years ago. And all I had to do was click the picture. My credit card info and address were saved in the app, my three-digit code memorized. And the kit was on sale FOR A LIMITED TIME ONLY! It was so easy, I didn't even have to think about it.

Fortunately, the kit was more money than I was willing to spend on an experiment in happiness, but I'll admit, they had me on that checkout page in less than a second, and it could've been on its way to my house before I had a chance to remember my bad hand-eye coordination extends to art.

Companies like PayPal, Apple Pay, Affirm, and more exist to make buying as quick and easy as possible. They capitalize on that anticipatory dopamine and have a receipt in your inbox before you know what happened.

It might seem like the world is a perfect storm of internal and external forces all in cahoots to get you to buy more and more. And you wouldn't be wrong, but it doesn't mean there aren't ways to weather that storm. And in weathering it, get closer to the things you want most in life.

DIY Dopamine Fast

For her patients with habits and addictions not at risk for life-threatening withdrawals, like gaming, smoking, and shopping, Lembke uses a dopamine fast as a way to retrain patients' dopamine receptors. Not just as a physiological solution but as a comprehensive study of a patient's entire journey with their addiction. She starts by collecting data, identifying the root causes for the addiction, and naming the problems the addiction is creating. At the end of the fast, she even works with them on next steps for incorporating the habit back into their life, if they want to, in a more manageable amount. The bulk of the dopamine fast is abstaining from the dopamine-triggering habit for a full month. Why one month? Lembke's research found an interesting phenomenon across many of her "fasting" patients. In the first two weeks, all her patients were miserable. The brain's reward pleasure pathways were starting to reprogram but weren't there yet. For patients abstaining from cannabis or sugar, their physical withdrawal symptoms peaked in the second week. After four weeks, though, the pathways were totally rewired and most patients reported positive experiences.

You can alter a lot in a couple weeks. Research shows that the brain's gray matter, which shrinks from alcohol abuse, begins reversing within just two weeks of abstinence, and 77 percent of athletes with mild traumatic brain injuries recover within four weeks.

In the grand scheme of things, one month is nothing. The average life expectancy of a woman in the US is around eighty years, which means one month is 0.1 percent of your life. But it could be the catalyst for reversing one hundred years of marketing manipulation. I (Jen) believe this because it happened for me. When Travis and I were paying off our debt, I had no sense of the word "moderation." I didn't think I had a spending problem (and I didn't want to change my spending), so I went all-in on side hustling to pay off debt faster. After two months of sixty-hour workweeks, at twenty-six years old I contracted shingles. I realized I wasn't going to be able to maintain that lifestyle long-term, so I needed to focus on both my income *and* my expenses. And because shingles taught me nothing about extremes, I decided to try a no-spend challenge. I joked that I'd done several involuntary ones in college, but they were less about saving money and more about not having any money. This time I wanted to save as much money as possible as fast as possible. Over two years I did three no-spend months. By the time we made our last debt payment, I'd learned more about myself and my spending from those challenges than I ever had before.

By abstaining from all non-necessary spending, I was able to fully focus on what was truly important. It was during my first no-spend challenge when I realized that going out with friends wasn't as much about the food as it was about the people. My no-spend challenges forced me to reexamine what I assumed I needed to spend on and get creative in how I met my needs.

Independent of Lembke's research, I found one month to be the sweet spot for initiating doable habit changes in my life. There are some great stories out there of people doing no-spend or low-spend years, and they're fascinating to read, but I wasn't trying to stop shopping for the sake of shopping. And a decade later, I still believe if your goal is to improve your spending habits without opting out of the system altogether, you don't need a whole no-spend year to learn that. Abstaining from nonessential spending for a month will allow you the space to focus on what's most important and rewire those reward pleasure pathways.

A quote I like from habit expert James Clear is "focus doesn't require a permanent no, but it does require a present no." Setting a thirty-day time limit to your no-spend challenge means you're not giving a permanent no to pleasure spending. You can and will go back to a lot of it. But a present "no" takes away some of the decision fatigue your brain experiences on a daily basis and gives you space to think more holistically about your spending decisions. With so much of our modern desire having been manufactured for us, taking a pause to consider what you truly love is an act of rebellion.

In 2017 I wanted to share with others what no-spend challenges had done for me, so I wrote a book titled *The No-Spend Challenge Guide* and published it on Amazon. And I had never dreamed of the response that little book would get. In seven years, the book has sold over twenty thousand copies and garnered over one thousand five-star reviews. In a world where personal finance books tell you to just stop spending money, the no-spend challenge is a way to learn what to stop spending money on. And it's working, at least for our readers:

"I have now been doing no-spend challenges periodically since reading and have been able to save, not only for myself but for my family, so we can enjoy more experiences together."

"I am saving more. I am spending intentionally. I am seeing results. My savings account balance is higher, and my anxiety level is lower!"

If you want to know the difference between what you truly love and the manufactured desires in your life, we think the single most effective thing you can do is a no-spend challenge, especially if you want to see results fast.

FedEx spent six years working on creating the first paperless cockpit, a system that would save them time and money and make many of their other projects easier to complete. They'd had this goal, planned for it, and allocated resources to it for more than six years, but with literally fifty other priorities competing for attention, it inched along. When FedEx decided to focus on this one thing, they got clear on what needed to be done, in what order, and rallied the team behind the plan. They had the system launched and in use in *two weeks*.

On any given day, there are thousands of decisions to make. With every decision competing for our attention, it's nearly impossible to figure out what you love and don't love spending money on. But if you commit for thirty days to having a singular focus on your spending, you could potentially gain years of progress in just a couple weeks.

How to Do a No-Spend Challenge

The goal of a no-spend challenge and a dopamine fast are the same: when you cut out or cut back on actions that give you a dopamine rush, you can retrain your brain to respond to those triggers less impulsively. The one rule of a no-spend challenge is straightforward: don't spend money on anything nonessential. But where there are rules, there are always exceptions. We've done many no-spend challenges ourselves and with our podcast listeners, and here are some of the exceptions and questions that come up every time:

"What if my car runs out of gas?"

First ask yourself, "Am I impulse buying gas?" and "Am I trying to meet a need with this gas that I could meet in another, less expensive or free way?" For the majority of people, the answers to these questions will be "no." Most of us aren't stress shopping at the pump. If your car runs out of gas, get more gas. Same with any number of necessary household items. The key is to build a habit of curiosity and ask those clarifying questions we talked about earlier (see pages 44-45). Even for necessary things like gas. Maybe asking the right questions inspires you to ask a coworker or neighbor to alternate carpooling, saving both of you money and the opportunity to get to know each other better. I can't tell you how many times I've heard a variation of the story "I tried a no-spend challenge, but I always end up buying [insert necessity], so I never completed it." Don't let perfect be the enemy of the good— come at this process from a place of curiosity.

"I'm waiting for a month where I don't have something to do."

That month will never come. And while we're on the subject, you also don't have to wait for the first day of the month. During the last no-spend challenge I did, we planned a trip to LEGOLAND. We have annual passes, so we go every other month to feel like we're getting our money's worth, and one month happened to fall on my no-spend challenge. Instead of postponing the start of the challenge, I used it as an opportunity to get creative and see how little we could spend. I packed sandwiches, snacks, drinks, the whole shebang. I made coffee at home and brought it with me in the car. And you know what? The only money we spent that day was on a hot dinner outside the park before we made the hour drive home. While I didn't have a total no-spend day, I wouldn't have been as motivated to not spend if I wasn't on the no-spend challenge. If you see a thirty-day window that you think is mostly good, schedule your challenge! And when those one or two days come up when you know you're going to spend, whether it's at a wedding, other event, vacation, whatever, challenge yourself to get creative with how or how much you spend.

"What if something I need goes on sale?!"

January is a popular month for our listeners to do no-spend challenges. When we surveyed them fourteen days in about what the hardest part was so far, we were shocked to hear how many people said "missing out on all the after-holiday sales." Sales deserve their own dedicated section in this book, and they will get it, but in the meantime, understand that sales are cyclical. It is extremely rare for an item to only go on sale once or even twice a year. Every time we get a good deal, dopamine releases in our brains and makes us feel smart. So, the next time a sale comes up, we want to take advantage of it so we feel smart again. Whether we need the product or not is of no concern to our brains, we just want to feel smart again. It's that dopamine reinforcement that makes it important to avoid sales while on a no-spend challenge. Now if it's something specific that you've been looking for for a while and it goes on surprise sale during your no-spend month, then sure, get it. But that scenario is far less common than we lead ourselves to believe.

"How do I get the most out of a no-spend challenge?"

So glad you asked. What we love about no-spend challenges is how customizable they are. There are so many ways to do one that results in positive change. But we get it, when there are too many options, deciding can be paralyzing. We're not here to stress you out more, so here's a flexible three-step method you can use to craft yours.

1. Prepare

Doing a no-spend challenge on a whim is setting yourself up for failure. While we don't think you need to wait for the first of the month or even a Monday to start, some prep work will help you get the most out of the challenge. First decide when you're going to do it and what you're going to cut out. You can choose to abstain from all nonessential expenses or just the three to four things you know are your biggest triggers.

While we consider groceries essential, some people take the opportunity to stay out of the grocery store by using the challenge to clear out their pantry stockpile or deep freezer. Whether you're planning to buy groceries during the challenge or not, make sure you're stocked on necessities like soap, toilet paper, diapers, anything you use regularly. Again, you *can* buy these things during the challenge, but it's helpful to prepare in advance if you know you'll run out in the next few weeks.

You'll also want to make a meal plan. We recommend making it for one to two weeks, but you may want to meal plan just once for the entire thirty days. Focus on meals that are easier (or almost easier) than ordering takeout. This isn't the month to start tracking macros or try Whole30. Focus on one challenge at a time. Last, you'll want to plan things to do. A no-spend challenge isn't a stay-at-home challenge. You know all those free activities you've been wanting to do? All those gift cards you've been hoarding? The hobby supplies you bought but haven't used yet? The free events sections of Facebook and Eventbrite? Go take advantage of them! This is the month to try new (free) things.

If this is your first no-spend challenge, we do recommend abstaining from all nonessentials to get the most out of it. A no-spend challenge allows you to remove the clutter of daily spending decisions so you can think clearly about your desires. The more exceptions you allow, the harder the challenge becomes, and the less you ultimately get out of it.

2. Abstain

Now it's time to practice. We say "practice" intentionally because that's what this is. Having a perfect no-spend month isn't the goal. During your no-spend challenge, take advantage of the space this short season creates to get curious. Here are some questions to journal about to better understand your spending habits. Record your thoughts while the events of the day are still fresh in your mind. Your notes will be a helpful resource to review once you've completed the challenge.

Each time the desire to shop comes up: What needs was I trying to meet by shopping?

What are the problems my unintentional spending has created?

What problems have unintentional spending held me back from solving?

What painful emotions is this challenge bringing up?

Am I judging myself for my performance during this challenge?

What are the next steps I want to accomplish with the knowledge I've gained from this challenge?

You'll also want to tell the people around you about your challenge. It'll be a little awkward, but trust us, it's worth it. I (Jen) posted daily to Instagram, and that's how people knew I was doing it. When I'd talk to a friend, they'd ask me how it was going, and one friend in particular who'd asked me out to lunch saw I was doing a no-spend challenge and, without my asking, suggested we do something else. I also wanted to get a coffee when I was with another friend, but she'd asked me about my challenge, so I felt like I couldn't buy something in front of her! My daily posting was meant to encourage others to stick with their no-spend challenges, but it had the unexpected benefit of helping me stick with mine.

Finally, tracking actions can help you see your habit change in a tangible way. Tracking helps you stay focused on your goal, provides rapid reinforcement of positive behaviors, and increases awareness of behaviors and patterns. If you're not tracking, you don't know if the actions you're taking are getting you to where you need to be. Many people try to track progress, but progress can be a disappointing and an uncontrollable thing to track. We love to see those cute grids and big thermometers fully colored in when someone pays off their debt, but if that's all you focus on, the months or seasons you color less, or can't color at all, may do more harm than good to your motivation. Tracking actions is much more gratifying than tracking progress. Unlike progress, you have total control of the actions you take and don't take, making it much more motivating to track. And it helps you take responsibility for your improvement as much as your mistakes (because we're far more likely to dwell on our mistakes than celebrate our success). You can also track them daily, maybe multiple times a day, so they're top of mind more often than a once or twice-a-month debt payment or savings transfer. Here are some examples of actions you can track:

Days you skipped takeout coffee
Meals you didn't get takeout for
Days you didn't make an unplanned grocery store trip
Days you ate dinner at home

The list goes on. But just because the list can be long doesn't mean your list should be. Intentional focus means honing in, so choose three to four actions that have the greatest impact on *your* spending. Your 90-day transaction inventory can help you get started determining what these actions will be. Once the no-spend challenge is over, you can continue tracking your three to four actions or create new ones based on what you learned throughout the challenge.

3. Reflect

You obviously don't need to wait until after the thirty days are over to reflect on your experiences. You'll think about and reflect on the decisions you make every day of the challenge, probably right before you go to bed. But after those first two weeks, you'll have a good amount of perspective to start thinking about what you did well, what was miserable, and remind yourself what all of this is really for. If you bought something you hadn't planned on, then come up with ideas and a plan that allows you to make a different decision next time.

Steve Jobs once said, "People think focus means saying 'yes' to the thing you've got to focus on. But that's not what it means at all. It means saying 'no' to the hundred other good ideas that there are. You have to pick carefully."

A no-spend challenge allows you the space (and excuse!) to say no to the hundreds of good ideas around you so you can train your brain to say yes to the things that matter.

When we reset our dopamine receptors, we can better identify the boundary lines of our capacities and resources, both internal and external.

⚡ **Lightning Round** ⚡

What are the manufactured desires that you're spending on in your life?

⚠

Action Step

Pick a day to start your thirty-day no-spend challenge and start preparing for it.

CHAPTER 5

Why We Impulse Shop

Two years ago, Travis and I (Jen) bought a fixer-upper. We spent two years renovating our home, and those years were some of the most stressful ones of my life. We slept in the living room for six weeks, the four of us shared one bathroom for six months, and we spent two months without a kitchen. On top of all that, we had a second baby, Jill and I published 175 episodes of *Frugal Friends*, and I wrote half of this book. I don't know if it was postpartum hormones or the handyman who lived in my guest room for several months, but my life felt out of my control. To compensate for the chaos at home, I'd make pit-stops at Starbucks for a little treat latte or take my sons to walk around the grocery store. Thankfully, we'd budgeted for some extra "stress spending" during the renovation. But when it was over and I didn't have the excuse (or the funds) to support my new coping mechanisms, I was a little embarrassed at how hard it was to return my spending to normal.

Change is hard, whether you're changing a habit you've had for years or a few weeks. It's exponentially harder when it's something you've been doing your whole life.

Whenever you stop or change direction, there's going to be friction. A lot of us hate the friction, but without it, it would be impossible to make the shift. Friction is the uncomfortable brush with reality that allows us to go in a different direction. A lot of people give up on doing new things because they forget that. We want our actions to change at the same pace our mind has changed, and we forget that changing direction doesn't happen instantly. We need to slow down first, and that requires friction.

When you move from spending on a whim to conscious consumption, there's a lot of friction. Not only have we and the people around us been told to desire in ever-increasing quantities, we also use shopping as an escape from and solution to many of our problems.

On your no-spend challenge, and when spending in general, the biggest obstacle you'll come up against is impulse spending, which is simply unplanned spending. It's deciding to buy something, then immediately buying it. A practice that is glamorized in media. I remember growing up watching actors on TV shows and movies making spontaneous purchases, saying things like "This round's on me boys!" to the whole bar and "Oh, what the heck, I'll take one of each!" to the boutique salesclerk. That's what I thought being an adult looked like, being able to spontaneously buy whatever you want.

When you Google "how to stop impulse spending," you'll get answers like "make a budget and stick to it," "reflect before buying," and "stick to a shopping list." These answers are simultaneously infuriating and hilarious, because if I could stick to a shopping list, I wouldn't be googling "how to stop impulse spending!" After a lifetime of being told to buy what you want when you want it, no one is showing their work on how to reverse that desire. And we kinda get it—it can be a complex topic. Impulse control and decision-making are run by several different parts of your brain. But in order to get to the root of why we impulse spend, we need to be looking at where impulse control comes from.

The part of our brain responsible for decision-making and impulse control is the prefrontal cortex. The prefrontal cortex operates slowly and is logical and precise. Unfortunately, our brains like to work quickly. It's a good thing overall, like in the instances of real danger where your survival brain kicks into that fight, flight, or freeze mode. It's great when a bear is about to attack you, but it's less helpful when you're trying to cut down on impulsive decisions. The limbic system is responsible for our survival brain, and it operates fast. Because of its correlation with keeping you alive, when dopamine is released, your brain prioritizes your survival brain. That's why a no-spend challenge is a great first step in stabilizing your dopamine receptor pathways. Because you can't truly "fast" from dopamine, and you don't want to—it's a vital neurotransmitter. While it rises in response to rewards, it doesn't decrease when you avoid them (i.e., no-spend challenge), so you must also focus on calming your survival brain down so your logical brain can get a word in.

We'll look at five of the ways the reward center of our brain (aka instant gratification) can overpower our logical brain and how to support our minds so we can make better real-time spending decisions.

Habit Spending

After college, our friend Paige got a job at a car dealership. She only worked there a year, but in that year she spent almost her entire paycheck, over $60,000 on . . . stuff. Clothes, accessories, handbags, anything she could buy at the mall. It started as a way to assimilate into her new identity as a working woman in the corporate world. "As silly and crazy as this sounds, I vividly remember thinking that I needed a closet that looked like Jennifer Garner's in *13 Going on 30* or Anne Hathaway's in *Devil Wears Prada*. I thought it was going to make me feel a certain way about myself. And it just didn't." She quickly realized that car sales were not for her. Buying her new work wardrobe was fun, though, so she kept going to the mall every day on her lunch break to escape the job she hated. She'd go four out of five days each week and buy something every time. After a year, it didn't even give her pleasure anymore, it was just a habit.

After going through your 90-day transaction inventory, you may have found quite a few purchases you have little to no memory of. I know I did. The latte I got on the way to see my mom, the lunch I got whenever I passed my favorite Chipotle, the beers I bought with friends when I didn't even really like beer! These purchases did absolutely nothing for me except continue a habit I didn't know I had. Habit change isn't easy, but it is a great place to start because most of these transactions, while they may have started as a way to purchase a new identity or escape a job you hate, after a while aren't tied to a deeper meaning.

If you've read any books on habits or ever Googled how to build better habits, you've probably been introduced to the Habit Loop: Cue → Routine → Reward. All our behaviors are triggered by a cue and followed by a routine that ends in a reward. Our brain remembers the reward, thanks to dopamine and the limbic system, and the next time it encounters the cue, the loop repeats. Eventually the behavior becomes habit, even if the reward loses its rewardyness.

We know now, thanks to the monkeys, that it's not the reward that elicits the most dopamine but the cue. So the easiest way to break this cycle is to catch it at the cue. If you eliminate, or hide, the cue, you can totally avoid the routine. And that means less willpower required to make values-aligned spending decisions. Here are some common cues:

Time: If you have a habit of shopping or buying something specific at a certain time of day, or even day of the week, that's a time-triggered purchase. For example, if I go to happy hour on Fridays or go to Starbucks every Double Star day.

Location: If you shop or buy something specific every time you're at a certain location, your purchase is triggered by location. For example, if I browse Amazon before bed, or I pick up a new shirt whenever I'm at Target, those are location-triggered spending habits.

Preceding event: Making a purchase every time you leave a certain place or event is a preceding event trigger. This also includes making a purchase whenever you're on your way to a place/event. For example, if I go out to lunch every Sunday *after* church or shop *after* every holiday sale. Or if I buy a new outfit *before* every vacation, or I buy new backpacks for my kids *before* every first day of school (whether they need them or not!), those are examples of preceding event triggers.

Other people: We have an innate desire to fit in with people. Usually it's people we like, but if we can't find those people, we'll take what we can get. That desire to belong can lead us to reflect the spending habits of those people, to no fault of their own. Like if I'm out shopping with friends and I buy something because everyone else is, or if everyone in the office is going out to lunch and I don't want to be the only one left behind. Those purchases are triggered by other people.

The bad news is that not every cue can be eliminated, but the good news is that a lot of spending habits have several cues, so you should have options. For Paige, work (location) triggered her desire to shop because she wanted to escape a job she hated. She realized that she was able to start fixing the root problem by looking for another job, but she didn't find one overnight. Thankfully, she also identified that lunchtime contributed to her habit of going to the mall. So, at lunch, she "escaped" the office in a different way. Instead of driving to the mall, she started taking her food to a nearby park where she read a book.

"There was one day, after doing this for a couple of months, when I was just sitting at the park, reading my book, I looked up and I felt a lot of peace. I remember thinking, I can't believe I used to go up to the mall every single day." Your spending habits may seem complex, but if you take some time to break them down, you'll find many of them just require a little creative tweaking to change.

Remember that spending as a result of any of these triggers isn't bad. But your brain loves efficiency, and it's creating habits whether you're aware of it or not. The more you allow these triggers to dictate your spending, the more you let them establish habits you probably wouldn't choose intentionally. When you're aware of the triggers, you take back control of what spending habits you practice.

Shopping as an Activity

Some people think society could benefit from experiencing boredom more often. Doing less would definitely save you more money.

We are not those people.

We love doing stuff.

Being bored is for boring people.

Just kidding, but our mission statement is literally "If it's not fun, it's not Frugal Friends," and we've been trying to convince you that frugality is fun since the first paragraph of this book!

Because we live by the principle of fun, we see and understand everyone who, like us, shops for fun. If you've ever hung out with friends at the farmer's market, strolled the shops downtown before your dinner date, or walked the aisles of the thrift store "just to browse," you are our people.

My childhood in the late '90s and early 2000s was defined by this. Every weekend my mom would take me to some kind of mall, big box store, or street event lined with local vendors. I can't recall my parents having hobbies. Shopping was our hobby. And we did it like it was a form of entertainment. When I wasn't out shopping, I was at home devouring the Alloy and dELiA*s catalogs, circling everything I wanted but that my parents would ultimately never buy me. A girl could dream!

While shopping looks different today, people still treat it as a leisure activity. Instead of thinking critically about boredom and healthy ways to spend our time, we can just pull out our phones and one-click-buy or get in the car and drive to Target. Picnicking in the park is free, but it isn't getting a lot of advertising, so it's not top of mind when we're thinking of things to do. Recently I saw an ad for a dollar sale at the local resale store and planned a group shopping trip with friends. I didn't need anything, it just seemed like a cool way to hang out with friends. I'm guilty of doing this at Sam's Club too. I know when they bring out the free samples, so sometimes I'll go just for the samples even though I know I'll inevitably walk out with something that was not free.

A growing number of scientists are actually devoting research to why we shop to overcome boredom. Processed healthily, boredom is your brain signaling for change. It indicates that a current activity or situation isn't providing engagement or meaning in hopes of provoking you to shift your attention to something more fulfilling. Processed unhealthily, boredom leads to impulsive decision-making.

Because of boredom's negative connotation, people who get bored easily are often undervalued in society. As children they're seen as immature, troublemakers, having short attention spans, and as adults their decisions can be seen as impulsive and irresponsible. First, if that sounds like you and you've ever been made to feel this way, we want you to know you are no less capable of success than people who don't "get bored" easily. Second, you have an edge that others don't. It may seem like a hindrance because a lot of traditional success involves conformity, but boredom can be your strength once you start pursuing healthy ways of responding to it.

So, what can you do if having fun for you requires spending money?

First, figure out the things you like that don't cost money! Half the battle is trying new things so you know what you do and do not like. We often spend money on a small group of activities that we know we like because we don't want to try something new that we may not like. But part of building your creative muscles is to do new stuff. Where deprivation requires giving up your needs, values-based spending requires getting creative in how you meet them. Not everything will be fun, and you don't have to force something to be fun for you because someone else likes it. I (Jen) personally hate thrifting. I love shopping second-hand online, but I hate hunting through thrift stores. Jill loves it! She lives for it! But as much as I wanted to love that activity, I had to lay it down and move on if I was going to fully live out values-based spending.

Second, you have to replace shopping with activities of equal effort and reward. If you tend to impulse shop on your phone before bed, then going for a run is not a suitable activity to replace it with. Instead, look for something fun you can do on your phone in your pajamas like playing a game, doing a language-learning app, or finding recipes for your next meal plan. Ultimately, it'll be up to you to decide the activities that give you a comparable dopamine hit. It's a good idea to make a list of things to try that are different "sizes." Scrolling on your phone or reading a book are small size. They require very low mental and physical effort. Here are some more small-size ideas:

Get a book from your library's app
Text a friend
Start a gratitude journal
Listen to a new album (or an oldie but goodie!)
Plan a bucket-list trip
Make a bucket list
Clean your email inbox
Organize and declutter your digital photos

Then there are medium-size activities that might replace shopping habits you'd leave your house for. Like it's late afternoon, I'm bored, and I want to experience the surreal joy of walking around Target or checking out Kohl's because they're having their famous "second week in August" sale. This is where you could replace shopping with something physical like going for a walk, run, or bike ride. Physical doesn't even have to mean exercise. You could also choose a hobby like knitting, coloring, or anything that requires you to move your body. Here are some other ideas:

Experiment with a new hairstyle
Call a friend
Declutter a drawer
Do a puzzle
Clean your car

Bake from scratch
Play a board game
Clean your jewelry or shoes
Look for a new job

Last, there are big activities. These are the outings you'd typically plan for, like semiannual sales, opening day at the farmer's market, or driving to the outlet mall. These can be replaced with big activities. Search your city's website for free events or volunteer at local events and concerts. Host a clothing swap when you want a closet refresh, host a Super Bowl potluck instead of throwing a full party or going out to a bar (this could be exchanged for any major event). Some other ideas could be:

Get tickets to a museum from the library
FaceTime a friend
Go to the pool or playground
Utilize an annual pass
Declutter a room in your house
Go for a bike ride or hike in a new place
Take your dinner alfresco or to a new place

Shopping as an activity isn't bad, if there is a shopping activity you truly value you can budget for it! But those tend to be the exceptions, not the rule. With a little planning, you can meet your brain's need for fun without spending money.

Stress Shopping

We're all facing unique personal challenges at home and work. Add to that the aftermath of a pandemic, intense global conflicts, polarizing politics, racism and racial injustice, inflation, and climate-related di-

WHY WE IMPULSE SHOP

sasters and it's no surprise that stress shopping is the number one impetus for impulse shopping. The American Psychological Association found that 36 percent of American adults said they don't even know where to begin when it comes to managing their stress.

Why does stress make us shop? One reason is our perceived sense of control. Feeling like there's something going on that you don't have control over will push you to do something that you *do* have control over, like choosing something to buy. When we said this in an episode of *Frugal Friends*, we got this response from a listener:

"Compulsive spending is such an issue for me. I've always tried to explain that shopping goes beyond the hit of dopamine. Control is the perfect word to use. I was thinking the other day, 'Winter is 3 months away. My kids need winter coats and I'll feel less stressed about them not having them if I just buy them now.' Then instead of taking the time to research and look for them secondhand or on sale I just immediately bought them. I always have this feeling of not being prepared, then buying something makes me feel more in control."

Another cause of stress spending is distraction. When you shop in person, the store can stimulate your senses, sights, and smells that distract you from stress. Even the act of simply scrolling or window shopping can release dopamine through the anticipation of buying a possible reward or treat. We're all for spending money to celebrate big wins like landing a new job, paying off your debt, or . . . writing a book. But when you think about rewarding yourself with a little treat, because, I don't know, you made it all day without buying yourself a little treat? It's time to reevaluate whether you're celebrating or distracting yourself.

So how do we overcome stress shopping? We treat the root cause of the shopping: the stress. We have to manage the stressors in our control and find healthy coping mechanisms for the stressors outside our control.

First, eliminate what you can. Simplify your schedule and surroundings (or whatever in your life feels complex) and ask for support during difficult seasons. If this feels like a big task, try giving your season an arbitrary end date. That way you can always go back to what you were doing before but you have an excuse as to why you need to cut out some things or get assistance for a period of time.

Next, find healthy emotion-focused coping mechanisms that work for you. These are true forms of self-care, and they don't have to cost money. They can even help in achieving some high-level internal needs. A good example is exercise.

Exercise allows us creativity to find a form of movement that works best for us, see a tangible example of our capacity for improvement, and can often be a place for building relationships. In a study to see what best alleviates stress hormones in the brain, mice were placed under stress and then given one hour per day of running on a treadmill. The results found that the exercise decreased anxiety-like behaviors immediately and improved their resilience to subsequent stressors in future tests.

Meditation is another. It strengthens our connection to a higher power and the world around us, and there's plenty of research that has established meditation as lowering resting heart rate and blood pressure, helping you sleep better, and helping you be more creative and patient (that alone will help you spend better!).

When our friend Brittany wanted to stop eating out (for health and spending reasons), she first recognized she was using it as a coping mechanism and then experimented to find a healthier one. "When something was making me anxious, I coped by making myself a little coupon book of stuff I liked that did not involve money or unhealthy food: a walk, twenty minutes at the library, a bubble bath, etc. It sounds so silly, but it actually worked!"

Again, experiment to find what works best for you. Here are a few more options to get you started:

Practicing art
Reading
Prayer

Playing sports
Spending time in nature
Spending time with friends

You need an arsenal of healthy coping mechanisms at your disposal, because while some are more powerful than others, those may not always be at your disposal when you need them. Remember, especially when these changes feel silly and uncomfortable, that impulse control comes from the brain. That means taking care of your brain will give you a better capacity to resist impulsivity, which leads to less impulse spending.

Social Influence

During our home renovation I (still Jen) followed a lot of interior design influencers on social media. I have little to no eye for design, but I'm also very picky. That basically translates to having a lot of opinions on other people's designs but not being able to come up with one of my own. Not a good combination. So, I was hoping these women, who could turn an empty room into a work of art with what I truly believe is sorcery, would help me articulate the design I wanted. The great thing about watching a ten-second video is that once the video is done the room is complete. But not once did anyone tell me how to figure out what "complete" is. I became overwhelmed trying to haphazardly re-create their perfect room, and because mine wasn't identical I didn't know when I was done. There was always one more picture or one more potted plant to buy.

When we strive for perfection, good is never good enough. Perfect curations on social media mean we're always buying the next thing to complete our lives to make them "perfect." One or two skin-care products aren't enough; you must have every product for every problem. One dress for spring is okay, but a haul of fifteen different dresses for the season is better! We know social media is a highlight reel, but that hasn't stopped it from fueling our perfectionism and the idea that the grass is greener on the other side.

But perfect doesn't exist. And even if it did, achieving it is nowhere on our list of internal needs. You can have everything you love with mismatched cutlery, an unaesthetic car, and laminate countertops. Water tastes great in the water bottle you already have, and a cozy blanket feels great on your couch, no matter how ugly you may think it is. The first step in overcoming socially influenced impulse spending is to stop wanting what other people have. No thing you can buy will make your life or home remotely close to perfect. So why waste money trying? Instead, maybe we start embracing an unaesthetic life. Stop being afraid of how our old dining table looks in pictures and celebrate all the times we get to share dinners on it with family and friends. Stop feeling bad about how simple our vacations are and start celebrating that we can afford to get away!

Some days we love using social media and others we want to delete it off our phones forever. It's difficult to find the radical middle. But like anything, neither extreme is the best option.

Setting physical boundaries can be a good action step to resetting how we think about ourselves in relation to what we see online. Taking a thirty-day fast or leaving your phone in another room for two hours each evening can be helpful. But no matter how good you feel about your social media usage, you will always be triggered to buy on the apps because that's a primary feature of their design.

Because of that, we've designed our not-patented two-step process for limiting social-media-influenced impulse buys (skip right to step two if you're already in a store!).

Step one: If the store website or app has the capability, make a shopping list called Impulse Intervention (you can actually call it whatever you want—this is just our favorite).

Whenever you want to buy something, add it to the list. If there is no list option, then create a note on your phone or in a journal.

This gives you an action to complete that gives instant gratification. We like adding it to a list instead of a cart because it keeps a barrier between you and buying. Stores remind you about forgotten items in your cart way more than on your lists, so putting it straight into your cart puts you at risk for an impulse checkout. Once it's on your list, wait at least forty-eight hours. Why forty-eight hours? If you bought something on Amazon Prime, it'd probably get delivered to you in about forty-eight hours, so if it works for Amazon, then we'll use it too. We've also seen people use one week, ten days, even a full month. We love the idea of scheduling a monthly shopping spree. You can choose one day each month to make all your impulse buys. That way you can see all the purchases you would've impulse bought individually in one cart and decide if that's how much you want to spend instead of finding out later that's how much you already spent. And if you truly want something, then you'll still want it in ten to thirty days, even if you miss a sale to do it. The number of items you'll pass up by saving and waiting to make a purchase will save you far more than any sale you'll miss out on!

Step two: If you're still thinking about this item forty-eight hours later, or you're already in the physical store, ask and answer these three questions before you buy:

How much will each use cost? We don't love rules, but we like the $1 use rule as a guideline. So, if something costs $20, will you use it at least twenty times ($1 per use?). If not, is it truly worth the cost? This can help you make your budget too. If you want to keep your clothes budget to $1 per wear, then theoretically you wouldn't need to spend more than $365 per year on clothes!

How long do I have to work for it? How many hours are you going to have to work to earn it? If you make $25 an hour, is a $100 pair of shoes worth half a day of work? This is an eye-opening question that you could ask with any transaction. Calculate how many hours you have to work to pay for your living and transportation expenses, then see if that $100 pair of shoes is worth four hours!

Is it filling a need? We often already have something at home that can serve the same purpose. Think first if you have something at home that can fill the need, even if it's not perfect, before you fill your home with more stuff.

It may be awkward and inconvenient to place these physical and time barriers to your shopping, but it's worth it, especially if comparison and perfectionism are stealing your joy (and money).

The Hunt

Finding a deal is the modern-day equivalent of hunting your own dinner. RetailMeNot found that two-thirds of consumers have made a purchase they weren't originally planning to make solely based on finding a coupon or discount, and 80 percent said they feel encouraged to make a first-time purchase with a brand that is new to them if they are offered a discount. Almost half said they would avoid brands that do not provide offers. Which sounds silly until you realize it's 100 percent true.

In 2012, Ron Johnson, the former head of Apple's retail stores, became the new JCPenney CEO. He immediately unveiled a sweeping overhaul to their marketing strategy: no coupons and discounts. Instead, he replaced them with "everyday low prices." No more gimmicks, just "fair and square" pricing.

Customers hated it.

Sales tanked nearly 25 percent in a year, and the company's stock plunged. Johnson lost his job after just seventeen months and JCPenney quickly brought back ~~deceptive pricing practices~~ sales and coupons. "We did not realize how deep some of the customers were into [coupons]," an executive said at the time. Johnson later agreed: "Coupons were a drug." And shoppers were addicted.

A former JCPenney employee said of the season: "I can't tell you how many people complained about not having coupons anymore.

They wanted to see the high prices getting lower at the register instead of just seeing a lower price. I never understood it."

That's because we want to believe we are getting more value for less money. Getting a deal may make you feel smart, like you've out-witted capitalism and you've gotta tell your friends all about it. In reality, thanks in part to JCPenney, stores know this. And their sales, discounts, and coupons are not for your benefit. A lot of them aren't even real.

Consumers' Checkbook, a nonprofit consumer-advocacy publica-tion, tracked product prices at two dozen major retailers for over six months. Researchers found that all but two companies used deceptive sales marketing. Retailers including Amazon, Walmart, JCPenney, and more had products "on sale" all thirty-three weeks or almost every week. This study expanded on studies they performed in 2015 and 2018. Every year shows deceptive sale pricing becoming more wide-spread across products and retailers.

Kohls has the audacity to say in their terms and conditions that they most likely never sold their sale items at their "original" price. They state: "The 'Regular' or 'Original' price of an item is the former or future offered price for the item or a comparable item by Kohl's or another retailer. Actual sales may not have been made at the 'Regular' or 'Original' prices."

These special-but-not-really discounts, holiday sales, and annual/semiannual/biannual/second-weekend-of-the-month events are de-signed to make you overvalue products, giving you a sense of urgency and scarcity of product, and discourage you from researching better offers or even better sales at other times of the year. After all, if it's "60 percent off" here, that's a great deal—why compare prices elsewhere?

So, there is no doable action step for this one. Maybe it's an anti-action step. Yes, we love finding a coupon or getting a bulk discount on something we were going to buy anyway, but buying something you "could" or "might" use simply because it's a good deal is a trick retailers are playing on you. Getting a deal is no longer a badge of honor. It's carefully played marketing. You know what's smart now? Only purchasing what you truly love and value, even if it's full price.

If you're wondering, the two companies that did not use deceptive pricing 100 percent of the time were Costco and Apple (who held no sales during the survey period).

⚡ Lightning Round ⚡

Which of the five reasons for impulse spending resonated with you most?

⚠️

Action Step

Revisit your 90-day transaction inventory and identify in what ways you see your "survival" brain overpowering your "logical" brain, causing you to impulse spend. It may be helpful to duplicate your spreadsheet and sort alphabetically by where the purchase was made. That way you can more easily see how often you're spending at each place. You can see an example of this in the video walkthrough on the resources page for this book at frugalfriendspodcast.com/book.

CHAPTER 6

Save Smarter, Not Harder

While there are many purchases we can say a complete "no" to, there are those physiological needs we can't totally opt out from. While we need to buy them, we'll often use their necessity as an excuse to over-spend on them. Without a clear-cut "no" drawing the line between what you do and don't value, it's really hard to figure out what to spend on these foundational expenses.

I (Jen) went into my last car purchase as prepared as I could be. I did my research, made sure I was only looking at the best makes and models from the last three to five years, and knew which dealer fees were required and which ones could be negotiated. I narrowed it down to two cars. One I was excited about, the other was just to say I didn't buy the first car I test-drove. They were the same price online, but one had lower mileage and the other had more premium features, and I really wanted adaptive cruise control. After test-driving the feature-laden car I intended to purchase, I sat down to negotiate. I knew about how much I could get shaved off the price, but what I was not ex-pecting were all the additional dealer fees. They even charged me a fee because my trade-in was over five years old! I negotiated the price for three hours and got them down quite a bit. But there were still so many fees they were unwilling to budge on. The longer I sat there, the more I felt I owed to the guy working with us. He was so nice and was trying everything he could. After three hours I was exhausted, late to pick up my son, and just wanted to be done. I had my heart set on this adaptive cruise control. I had the pen in my hand to sign the deal and realized the quote I got for the other car was $4,000 less. I was about to pay $4,000 for adaptive cruise control and leather seats . . . because I was tired. I thought, if I wanted it that bad, I could get it installed for less than that. And I don't even care about leather. Walking away from that showroom was physically painful. All that time and effort was spent for nothing. But we immediately picked up my son, went to the other dealership where the price they showed online was the price they charged, and got the van with less mileage for $4,000 less than I was about to pay. I negotiated to the best of my ability, but what saved me the most money was that I was willing to say no when the negotiations were not going in my favor.

One decision saved me $4,000. So much of the conversation on saving money is centered around how many things you can do to save money. The more things you do, the more you save, right? In reality, there are a thousand $4 decisions I no longer have to worry about simply because I was intentional with this one. That's why when we think about spending on needs, we take a less is more approach. How can we save as much as possible by doing as little as possible?

The Vital Few and the Useful Many

In 1906, economist Vilfredo Pareto noticed that 80 percent of Italy's land was owned by roughly 20 percent of the population. He then researched land ownership in a variety of other countries and found, to his surprise, a similar distribution in each. In 1941, engineer Joseph Juran came across Pareto's work and found it applied to quality issues. He found that once you find the 20 percent of causes that make up the majority of your quality issues, you can save a lot of time and effort by always trying those first. Most people call it the $80/20$ rule, but Juran referred to it as "the vital few and the useful many," to remind us that while we should start with the most important 20 percent, the remaining 80 percent of causes shouldn't be ignored. We found that most of the frugal living content out there focused on the "useful many," rebate apps, coupons, deals, etc. And while all those things are useful, we want to start with the vital few. Instead of stressing yourself out with a hundred things you need to do to save $4 here and $50 there, start with the few actions that can save you the most money, then incorporate the "useful many" at a rate that feels good to you.

Saving money in this way takes the pressure off doing values-based spending perfectly. Sure, it would be great if you knew everything you valued and spent on it fully 100 percent of the time. But that's never going to happen, and that's too much expectation to put on yourself. Making one or two of the right vital spending decisions annually or quarterly will make a massive difference in your finances, so you won't have to stress as much about the daily decisions of smaller purchases.

The Big Three

So, what are the vital few? Every year the Bureau of Labor Statistics takes a Consumer Expenditure Survey (CE). The survey provides data on expenditures, income, and demographic characteristics of consumers in the United States. There are, not surprisingly, just three categories that make up 64 percent of total household spending outside of savings and retirement investing. They are:

Housing: 33%
Transportation: 17%
Food: 14%

Housing and transportation alone make up half of the average American's expenditures every year. You could buy a latte every day, never use a coupon, and pay full price for everything and you'll probably still save more money annually if you saved intentionally on just your car and home expenses. But how? On most budgets, the first section for expenses is often labeled "fixed expenses." Somewhere along the line, we've interpreted "fixed" to mean that the expense can't be changed. So, we live with the big fixed expenses and lower all the tiny variable expenses. "Fixed" doesn't mean the expense can't be changed, just that it doesn't vary much from month to month. Expenses in other categories can be lowered or increased at will, but fixed expenses are changed less frequently. That's because we're not buying houses, cars, or appliances every year. Because they're infrequent, we think they don't matter as much. On the contrary, just because we're not making these decisions every year doesn't mean those choices don't matter. They are the choices that matter most.

Every year you're likely to make some kind of significant housing or transportation decision. They're difficult to align with your values because there are so many factors going into one decision. But if you take your time with these big decisions, they make future smaller decisions easier or unnecessary. Luckily, there isn't a laundry list of decisions—80 percent of the time it's going to be one of these three:

Housing

Your mortgage or rent is your biggest expense month over month. If you don't own a home, the biggest housing decision you might be facing is "Should I buy a house or keep renting?" If you're a renter and want to continue renting, you have the most flexibility in lowering your monthly housing cost. You can negotiate your rent every year, but you can also live literally anywhere and move whenever you want. I (Jill) found the "third option" within this category by living in an RV for a few years. This allowed Eric and me to own within our means and reduce our living expenses significantly.

Now, your job, family, etc. may limit the ability for you to live in a vehicle like we did, but that doesn't negate flexibility. You can test out living somewhere new or in a smaller place for a year at a time, save some money, and if you don't like it, you can change. No decision is permanent, and you don't know what's gonna work for you until you try. If you're a renter looking to buy, then you have some extra questions to answer:

How long do you want to stay in the area?

Do you know how much square footage you need or are you guessing?

How much renovation do you want to do? And are you willing for the renovation timeline to be double your initial estimate?

Can you afford your own independent comprehensive inspection? (because you probably need it!)

Do you need to own in the "best" school district? Have you toured the schools in the more affordable districts?

How much have insurance and property taxes risen in the area in the last ten years, and how does that compare to other areas?

Do you want a homeowners association (HOA), and at what rate are those fees increasing?

There is no right answer, but when you make a decision this big based on feelings, assumptions, and other people's opinions, you risk wasting a lot of money. A 2024 study found that renting is less expensive than buying in the fifty largest metros in the US. That won't always be the case, but it is the case now and will likely be the case again sometime in the future. In 2023, mortgage interest rates crested to their highest level in decades and home sales declined to the slowest pace since the Great Recession. Owning a home is a great financial decision, but it's not the best decision for everyone. If the numbers don't work for your income and lifestyle, then it's not wise to force it.

Say you do go into the home buying process, and you decide on a $300,000 budget, but after a few tours you realize the homes are not what you had in mind. So, you start looking at the $350,000 homes, and they are leaps and bounds better. An extra $50,000 will cost you about $300 extra per month. A realtor might say, "It's just $300 a month, it'll be worth it, you'll make it back in equity." But consider that

$300, no matter where it's going, is $300 you can no longer spend on anything else. It will be promised to your mortgage company for the next thirty years or until you earn enough equity to refinance. That's a $70 date night every week, a $3,600 summer vacation, or two $1,800 trips you won't get to take every year. It's $3,600 more you'll have to earn doing a side hustle to pay down debt or afford the things you love. It's $108,000 you won't be able to invest over thirty years, which, with 6 percent compound interest is potentially $365,000 you lose out on in retirement. What else can you cut from your budget that's going to save you $365,000?! And that $50,000 may cost you even more if you then have to put essential purchases on a high-interest credit card. While $50,000 might not seem like much in the short-term, this one decision will save you more than every discount code and cup of coffee you make at home.

If you already own a home, it's much harder to get that $50,000 back once you've spent it. But if you bought pre-2020, you're in a much better position. Your biggest housing expense will likely be replacements, upgrades, and renovations. Like we talked about in the last chapter, in today's social media culture, it's easier than ever to scroll through the beautiful kitchens and living rooms of influencers and feel inferior because no one would want to film a recipe video on your countertops and your shiplap is years out of style. There are renovations that boost the value of your home and there are renovations that keep up with trends. Make sure you're doing the ones that will have a return on investment. Don't waste thousands of dollars on handmade tile or removing a load-bearing wall for an open concept style that's already becoming outdated. Do the upgrades and renovations that are best for your family, not your social media posts.

Transportation

For many Americans, the cost to finance a vehicle will be the second biggest hit to their wallet each month after housing. The frugal transportation choice used to be buying cars in cash, but with new car prices up 29 percent since March 2020 and used car prices up 34 percent, that advice is no longer feasible for most people. As cars become more expensive at an alarming rate, auto loans help us afford a safe vehicle even if we haven't saved enough for one. But again, a small difference in the short-term can make a big impact in the grand scheme of your spending. Currently, the average loan for a new car is around $40K with a monthly payment of $729. The average loan for used cars is $26K with a monthly payment of $528. And don't let those low new car interest rates fool you. Even though used cars have a higher average interest rate than new cars, because the average used car price is so much lower, buying used saves you $200 per month on the same loan length. That means this one decision can save you $200 each month. That's over thirty-three lattes a month. By purchasing a used car just three to five years older than the new one you wanted, you can buy a $6 latte every single day and still be spending less than if you'd bought the new car.

But, guys, what if my car breaks down? I lease my car because I don't want to worry about maintenance!

First of all, a three- to five-year-old car shouldn't be breaking down, and dealers usually include no-cost warranties on the mechanical parts that make the car go. You can also upgrade to a warranty for the tech stuff so you don't have to worry about it. So, think about what you really need if your car is in an accident or does break down for some reason. Is it worth $200 per month? At the time of this writing, a Premier AAA membership costs less than $200 a year for two people and gets you two hundred miles of towing, free fuel delivery, battery jump-start/ boosts, mobile battery service, vehicle locksmith up to $150, extrication/ winching (if you get stuck in a ditch or inclement weather), flat tire replacement, on-site repairs, and even bicycle roadside assistance. A dealer will rarely if ever do any of this, regardless of whether the car is new or leased. And most lease agreements only cover repairs under factory warranty and will still require you to pay for excess wear and tear. If that's what you're concerned about, you can still find many three-year-old used cars with mileage low enough to be within bumper-to-bumper warranty for at least the first couple months, not to mention additional warranties offered on certified pre-owned cars.

Another big barrier for some people who choose to lease or buy new is safety and reliability. It's a concern for those of us who buy used as well. Cars usually depreciate anywhere from 15 percent to 20 percent in the first year. So even buying a one- or two-year-old car will get you most of the latest safety and efficiency features while saving you money. After five years cars fall to around 40 percent of the original price. For us, that's the sweet spot we like to buy in, anywhere from three to five years old with 10,000 to 14,000 miles per year. People also tend to buy like they're going to own the car forever. Even if that's what you hope to do, buy with resale in mind so you can identify better deals. For instance, if car A costs $2,000 more than car B, B obviously saves you $2,000 immediately. Before you buy, check what both cars will be worth in seven to ten years. If car A is a more reliable brand, it may be reselling for $2,500 more than B, making car A the better deal long term (by potentially $500).

Before you buy a used car, check out sites like CarComplaints. com to see the most common complaints for every vehicle make, model, and year. And find a free car depreciation calculator online to compare the resale values of any vehicles you're interested in.

Just as important as the price and quality of the vehicle is to be cautious of where you buy your vehicle. Dealerships have gotten a lot better about pricing transparency, but it's still up to you to find the dealers who charge what they say they're going to charge and avoid the ones who will try to slip $4,000 worth of fees under your nose.

And that leads us to our last point. You may want all the bells and whistles, but ask yourself, "Would I pay to add this if the car didn't already have it?" You can swap out the head unit to a unit with a screen, add a backup camera, upgrade the speakers, and even add adaptive cruise control to any car. I looked it up later, and adaptive cruise control costs about $2,000 to add. I wouldn't pay $2,000 for it, and I'm definitely glad I didn't pay $4,000.

Food

We put out requests for episode ideas several times a year. The requests we get the most, by a landslide, are related to saving money on food. Because while housing and transportation decisions save you more overall, you're only making those decisions every couple of years. We make food decisions every day, multiple times a day, sometimes multiple times an hour . . . because food is delicious. Food also brings people together, it enriches the travel experience, it heightens the senses, and fuels creativity. It's why food is one of the top areas of impulse spending we all face and why the more intentional you are with your food choices, the better you'll get at values-based spending in all other areas. So how do we make those decisions that give us 80 percent results with 20 percent effort? That could be a book in and of itself (and maybe it will be???), but just in case that book never gets written, here are the two routines we practice every week to make sure we're being efficient with our food spending and use.

1. Meal Planning

When Travis and I (Jen) were paying off debt, we were renters and had paid off cars, so meal planning was the one change I made that had the biggest impact on my spending. Before that, I would just go to Publix, walk the aisles, and let the grocery store tell me what to make. I stuck to generic brands and looked at price per ounce, but I always came home with random things that I would use once and not know how to reuse. Things sat in my pantry that I had high hopes for in the store, but in real life I was too busy to make. Now, I walk into my kitchen, let my fridge and pantry tell me what to make, write a list for the rest, and no one in my house has to ask me "What's for dinner?"

If you've ever tried meal planning and been unsuccessful, you may be trying to fit a round peg in a square hole. Don't worry, there's a space that fits for you in meal planning. There are two types of meal planners: Jens and Jills.

Some people, like Jen, love planning. We want to create the perfect meal plan every week with healthy meals. We want variety and the best utilization of every ingredient. The pro for Jens is that meal planning comes naturally to you. The con is that you often don't follow through with your perfect meal plan because life isn't perfect. We don't live in a vacuum. You may have planned for a forty-five-minute meal on Wednesday, but by the time it rolls around, you only have the energy for a fifteen-minute meal, but you made that one on Monday. Your goal is to give up having the best meal plan and pursue a realistic meal plan. Look at your week and be honest about the days you have time and energy and the days you don't. And know that it's totally okay if seven out of seven are "no time, no energy" days. Those seasons happen, especially with kids. Prioritize short ingredient lists, little to no prep time, and as few dishes as possible. Every week I do some version of a one-pot chicken and rice, a freezer meal (sometimes prepared in advance by me, sometimes store-bought), and a salad. After years of cooking, those are dishes I've found that I'll say yes to before saying yes to takeout. Your goal is to find yours.

If you're not a planner, meal planning can still be for you, just in a different way. Other people, like Jill, want flexibility. Maybe you travel a lot or you don't want to tie your schedule down to a recipe in case something else comes up. Or you love to cook and want the freedom to try new ingredients. The idea of a rigid meal plan and grocery list may sound horrible to you. Or at best unrealistic. The solution for you is an options list. Each week Jill takes inventory of what she already has on hand and meal options that can be made with those ingredients. Because she and Eric both work from home, this plan includes a list of four or five lunch options and four or five dinner options. When mealtimes roll around, she uses this like a menu and decides what sounds good in that moment. Since these options will often include shelf staples or items in the freezer, it's no biggie if a meal doesn't get made, it can just be made another day that week.

The goal of your meal plan isn't to take away spontaneity, it's to prevent those extra trips to the store to pick up something you need plus three more things you didn't. It's to prevent emergency take-out, not just at dinnertime but for breakfast and lunch. Skip the rigid plan and opt for a meal outline. You may not get excited to inventory and categorize every ingredient in your kitchen, so just create a list of options. Start with things you make often that you know you love, foods that you'd easily make before getting takeout. Consider those your pantry staples, and always have the ingredients for those things on hand, keep your freezer stocked with zero-prep meals, and commit to only one grocery store trip per week. If you want a more structured outline, try theming each day by cuisine or protein. Mondays can be Italian or meatless, Tuesdays Mexican or chicken, etc. It gives you a little guidance without feeling restricted.

If, even with a plan and a list, you're still prone to impulse spending at the grocery store, then try not going. I discovered this trick when I had my first son and he was not into grocery shopping. Ever since then, I've grocery shopped online. I quickly realized how much better I stuck to my list when I didn't go into the store. And now I do it because it saves me from *his* impulse purchases! Every Saturday before bed I head to the kitchen, identify the things that need to get used up and the things I'd like to use, and plan my meals for the week. I then buy groceries straight from my phone and pick them up Sunday afternoon. I also add things straight to my cart throughout the week as soon as I realize we're low. It has cut down on so many extra trips to the grocery store. I only have to step foot into a physical grocery store once or twice a month. It saves me time, money, and the mental energy of deciding whether to impulse buy.

I could go on about meal planning, but there's a key element that, if missed, makes your meal plan irrelevant. That key? Following through with the plan. If you don't follow through with your meal plan, then you'll spend all the money you saved, and then some, on takeout and dumping spoiled groceries in the trash. The second routine is the 20 percent effort that solves that problem 80 percent of the time.

2. Meal Prepping

Meal planning changed my buying, but it was meal *prepping* that changed my cooking habits. I (Jen) had the planning part down, but the execution was poor. When I started prepping, I filled in the gaps that meal planning just wasn't cutting. Now, when I say meal prep, I don't mean glass containers lined up on a kitchen island with a week's worth of meals perfectly portioned and positioned or mason jar salads that have always seemed impractical. I mean ingredients. Take shredded chicken, for example. I love it in soups, tacos, salads, beans and rice, and more. But the extra effort it takes to shred it with forks is a deal breaker for me. I'd rather order takeout. So, I started buying big bags of frozen chicken, cooking it, shredding it with my stand mixer, and freezing it in individual containers. Before it took me almost five minutes to hand-shred a pound of chicken; now I can do five pounds in less than thirty seconds. And cooking time is down for all my recipes because the chicken is precooked. Shredded chicken was a barrier to following through with my meal plan, and since I didn't want to eliminate it, I got creative and took the barrier away. Another barrier for me was chopping onions. Who doesn't hate chopping onions? So instead of eliminating them, because that would eliminate *a lot* of recipes, I prepped them. Now I buy a bag of onions, chop all of them in my $20 Ninja Express Chop, and freeze in individual containers. Whenever a recipe calls for an onion, I just grab a bag and drop it into the pan, no defrosting required. These are just my examples. Over time you'll identify what your barriers are and get creative with how you get past them.

When you're trying to lower your food spending, remember that a few of the right decisions here can free you from so many other decisions later. And even small steps in the right direction make big impacts. If your goal is to lower your spending this year and you had to choose between lowering your monthly food spending by 10 percent or your clothing spending by 50 percent, which would you choose? Probably 10 percent on food, right? According to the Bureau of Labor

Statistics, they both equal around $1,000 annually. So, there's no need to try to massively overhaul your food budget. Just focus on making small changes in the right direction.

⚡ Lightning Round ⚡

What's a housing decision you can make in the next ten years to lower your total cost of housing?

What's a transportation decision you can make in the next five years to lower your total cost of transportation?

What's a food decision you can make next week to lower your total cost of food?

Action Step

Write a meal plan that you can commit to following through with 100 percent for one week. Don't focus on making it the healthiest, best-looking, or least expensive. Prioritize follow-through.

Don't Go Broke

CHAPTER 7

Simplify Your Environment

Welcome to part 3: "Don't Go Broke."

By now, you're getting familiar with your values, spending behaviors, and some of the sub-skills that will help you improve your spending. And if it's taken you more than a day to get to this part, you've probably already started identifying some purchases you feel good about and some you don't. It's here in part 3 that we're giving you the principles you need to stick with the process.

While going broke can happen a lot more quickly than getting rich, neither happens overnight. The lifestyle you choose to embrace, the people you surround yourself with, and the mindset you adhere to each play a major role in whether you choose values-aligned spending decisions or impulsive ones.

The key to sticking with values-based spending long-term is embracing how your brain works. We're all prone to try to go all-in on good changes, but sometimes what looks good is unrealistic. We can say "no more impulse buys" all day, but our brains crave instant gratification, and the moment we have a stressful day, our brain forgets what it wants and goes for what it needs in the moment: dopamine. Now that we know how our brains work thanks to the last section, we can talk about how we can use our knowledge to our advantage to keep up beneficial money practices long-term. Or, hopefully, just long enough for values-based spending to become second nature.

The biggest thing that derails people's progress toward change is unexpected obstacles. We wish we could do something about that for you, but we can't. We do know that having an emergency fund and other savings accounts can make these obstacles a lot easier to deal with, but we can't take them away entirely. All we can do is give you the same encouragement we give ourselves: "Focus on the things that are in your control and learn to expect the unexpected."

We're not saying to expect bad things to happen, but know that your journey will constantly alternate between smooth seasons and seasons of friction. All we can do is curate the environment that we have control over in hopes of minimizing as many self-imposed obstacles as possible. Part 3 is dedicated to talking about curating your external environment, relationships, and mindset in a way that will support your new spending skills and habits.

Curating our internal and external environments is like wearing a coat on a walk in the fall. You could definitely take a walk without one, but it probably wouldn't be as long or as enjoyable as if you were wearing one. And every gust of wind would feel much more like a personal attack. By now you know and understand values-based spending, but without any support you probably won't practice it very long, and that first unexpected obstacle is definitely going to feel like a sign to quit. When you focus on environment, you stand a much better chance of making these changes last. And the easiest place to start is your external environment.

This includes the ways you refine the world around you to support your values-based decisions. Should you add more self-care routines into your schedule or reduce the number of weekly commitments you have? Should you get more organizational bins to manage what's in your closet or give away what you don't use anymore? To figure out how most people would answer these questions, a group of researchers at University of Virginia conducted a study to find out how people tend to solve problems that require creative thinking. Do we err on the side of adding or taking away? After a series of experiments with over a thousand participants, they found that no matter the problem at hand or the incentives provided, people tend to default to adding things to solve their problems. No more than 40 percent of participants on any experiment ever chose to subtract or simplify to solve it, even on problems where the subtractive option was the only right solution. The study showed that our brains err on the side of more when problem-solving. We are more likely to do or add more to solve problems rather than take something away, which is why it's so easy to get us to buy stuff! And it's a contributing factor to why life and our environment feel so complex.

Choosing Complicated

This tends to be the default for us for many different reasons. Sometimes we attach value to being busy. We can feel more important if we're productive, which can also be tied to a deeply rooted fear of disappointing others or ourselves.

Another explanation for our propensity toward complicated is a little something called complexity bias, a common cognitive bias that predisposes us to prefer complex solutions over simple ones. In the case of complexity bias, we skip over an easy fix or explanation, assuming it must be more nuanced and intricate, so we'll select "complex" even when we don't need to. This happens in all aspects of our lives from product purchases and relationship statuses to investment choices. It's especially interesting because biases exist as an effort to *save* mental energy, and yet, unfortunately, when left unchecked, they can cost us.

One of the most harmful consequences of complexity bias is our tendency to refuse to learn new things because we think they're going to be too complicated. This is me with anything tech or computer related. Literally anytime something is not working "how it should," I melt into a puddle and immediately call it IMPOSSIBLE! Until I decide to just turn it off and turn it back on again. Problem solved.

We also see this bias crop up when it comes to investing. It feels over-whelming. There are acronyms we don't understand. There are even people whose job it is to tell us it's complicated, so we pay them to invest for us.

Marketers also know this about human psychology and will take full advantage of it to make a sale. In the toiletries section of the store I (Jill) saw products boasting "microbiome nutrient serum" and "100 percent pure unrefined first-pressed." Few of us actually know what the heck all that means, and our lack of understanding leads us to believe "It must be good! Imma buy that!"

Complexity bias leads us to *prefer* complex solutions over simple ones. The trouble with choosing complicated is that our brains prefer simple. It's why cognitive biases exist in the first place! For example, when sixty women were asked to give a tour of their home, the ones who believed that their home was cluttered had increased cortisol levels in response to the request and were more likely to feel constantly tired and exhibit symptoms of depression. Another study found that participants who felt they had a chaotic kitchen made poorer food choices than those who felt they were in control of their kitchen.

Our propensity toward complexity fills our daily lives with thousands of little things to think about. What to eat, what to wear, who to call, or where to go, all of it piles up, taking precious brain space and pushing out or making other, possibly more important, decisions overwhelming. It's called decision fatigue, and when this happens, it leads us to choose the path of least resistance, which usually costs money.

We think of our mental capacity like a balloon. The air we blow into that balloon is all the daily demands, choices, and considerations of life. There's room for quite a bit of air, and some people's balloons are able to hold more than others. But something that all balloons have in common is that eventually, when filled too much, they pop!

We've all been there. Overextending beyond our capacity and "popping." Whether in the form of lashing out, shutting down, giving up, abandoning plans, or powering through despite detriment to ourselves. It happens. But even worse than popping, we often don't solve the problems that got us there in the first place. We just grab another balloon and keep filling it with the same type and amount of air, hoping this time this balloon will be limitless. They never are.

Instead, what if we learned to operate within the confines of that balloon? To become familiar with our capacities, know what's enough, what's too much, and how to let some of that air out every once in a while?

When we can find room for making decisions simpler, eliminate unnecessary choices, and decrease complexity, the less likely we are to pop. Instead of choosing complexity that leads to stress spending and burnout, what if we intentionally committed to simplicity?

Choosing Simplicity

The perks of simplification are endless. At its core, simplifying aims at maximizing the things that are valuable and minimizing the things that are wasteful. When applied to all areas of our lives, we can experience less stress, greater efficiency, and more of what we enjoy.

The trouble is, despite the knowledge of these benefits, we can be drawn to complexity instead. And without systems of maintenance in place, the whole thing can become expensive, complicated, or chaotic.

For example, take when my husband, Eric, and I (Jill) were living in our RV. As part of the full-time RVer world, we learned that there's quite the spectrum of approaches to the lifestyle! We lived in a motorhome to reduce our living expenses, but others did it to explore the country comfortably. They had brand-new motor coaches with king-sized beds, quartz countertops, multiple bathrooms, and full outdoor kitchens that pulled out from the side. All on wheels! For us, it cost very little, but for others, this same lifestyle was a multi-million-dollar endeavor. We had friends and acquaintances interested in the lifestyle, for both money-saving and adventure-seeking reasons, who asked us about building out vans and buses. Our common response became "There's a way to do it complicated and expensive, and there's a way to do it simply and inexpensive." And this is true for nearly every category of life. We can make our schedules, relationships, environments, and finances complicated or simple.

Now when we say simple, we don't mean plain or boring. We're not advocating for minimalism or stoicism for the sake of simplicity. We want you to think of simplifying as taking an intentional subtractive approach instead of the automated additive solutions we're used to.

Simplifying isn't always the right answer—sometimes rearranging or reprioritizing is—but it's hard to see what the answer is in the clutter of complexity we've built around our lives. So, in order to get a grasp on our external environment, here are three places we can start simplifying:

Our physical spaces, schedules, and routines.

Physical Spaces

We recommend beginning with simplifying your physical space because it's the most tangible category, and it can have a profound impact on the rest of your life. And since our minds are the beginning place for our actions, we're going to emphasize some of the reasons simplification is a good idea.

Less clutter = less stress. When there's stuff all over my (Jill's) home, my senses are heightened (whether or not I'm fully aware of it). The stuff demands my attention, whether or not I have the time to give it. From "clean me" to "fix me" to "organize me" to "use me," the stuff calls out. And sometimes I respond, "Not right now," or "Okay, right now, even though I've got five other more important things to do," or "Gotta put that on the list," or "one-click buy that replacement." And all these little conversations with my things turn into less room for conversation with my people. I am more likely to disproportionately react to stressors and experience tension inside myself and irritation with others. Alternatively, when there are fewer or simpler things to maintain and use, I feel calmer, I'm not as distracted, and my energy isn't depleted by all the physical clutter.

Less time and energy spent cleaning and organizing. When I was younger, I loved collecting things. Candle snuffers, tiny boxes, and snow babies (if you don't know what these are, it's worth the internet search so you can laugh along imagining eight-year-old Jill fawning over these creepy ceramic figurines). I would often show my Gimba (what I call my grandma) my new trinkets.

She would say, "Do you know what I call that? Dust collectors!" At the time, I thought it was such a buzzkill, but as I get older, I hear her words more and more in my own voice. I don't want stuff because I don't want to clean it! And because those dang Beanie Babies, Pogs, and rock collection never actually held their value despite all the promises.

When you simplify your physical space, you also have the opportunity to redefine your meaning of "enough." This is different for every person, but without it you will flounder to know where your satisfaction lies. As you work to find, make room for, spend, and live out of your values, you will be closer to a life of contentment and, by proxy, one of simplicity.

Knowing what's enough is a process, and your definition will continuously be refined throughout your life, but when this is your aim, you can Goldilocks this thing and designate what's too hot, what's too cold, and what's juuuust right.

You will need to engage with all the "too much," possibly finding what's "too little" in order to eventually land on "enough."

Since we love gamifying things, we've found various declutter challenges to be effective in helping us to simplify our physical environment. A few of our favorites are:

The 30-Day Declutter: For one month at least one item is intentionally removed from the home each day either via donation, selling, recycling, or trash. For an extra challenge, increase the number of items removed each day (i.e., day 1: declutter one item, day 2:

declutter two items, and so on). This intensified strategy will lead to 465 items removed from the home over the course of the month.

The 12-12-12 Challenge: This involves moving through your entire home searching for twelve items to donate, twelve items to put in their proper place, and twelve items that need to be tossed.

The 10 Spaces, 10 Items, 10 Minutes Challenge: This requires only spending ten minutes in one space (room, closet, maybe even just one kitchen cabinet!) and decluttering at least ten items. We like this one because it doesn't need to be accomplished in one sitting! This could be an undertaking over the course of a few weeks.

As we're removing all unnecessary stuff from our spaces, we can also be taking inventory of the type of clutter collectors we are. Similar to looking at our 90-day transaction history, you can look at your things and identify what category most of it falls under. Whether it's aspirational, sentimental, straight-up trash (that you thought was treasure), freebies, or sale items that you never truly needed, too much of a good thing (looking at you, bulk buys and duplicate toys), or "someday I'll have a use for this" odds and ends. Knowing your clutter kryptonites can help you learn more about what you don't value and stop spending on them.

We also want to note that we're not shedding stuff for the sake of minimalism. We're not getting rid of clutter because minimalism is some virtue to attain or to acquire this one version of a minimalist aesthetic but because we want peace in our space and minds. And we want our future spending decisions to be informed. It's possible that we could spend tons of time, energy, and resources maintaining a version of minimalism but sacrifice "simple" in the process. That's why we like to think about pursuing simplicity over just getting rid of stuff or obsessing over a lifestyle. You can have stuff and still have a simple life. You just have to define what that looks like for you.

Schedules

Once we've simplified and refined our physical space, we also need to look at our schedules and be honest about what's working and what's not. One of the biggest mishaps in our language is the term "time management." We can't manage time, we can only manage ourselves in the midst of time. Maybe it's just semantics, but we pack our schedules and to-do lists as if the term is taken literally.

Yet when we can effectively manage ourselves and our schedules, we reap the rewards of:

Time for ourselves. When it comes to self-care, we can struggle with feelings of selfishness or lack of deservingness, but the reality is we can only be the best version of ourselves for others when we've had space to meet our own needs. Whether it's taking a nap, gratitude journaling, participating in a hobby, or exercising creativity, it's carving out space in our schedules for these things that are life-giving and help us to show up for others as our best selves.

Richer connection. When we're not bogged down, busy, or distracted, our time with our loved ones can be more meaningful. When there's less to worry about or activities cluttering our calendar, we can enjoy the present moment and more fully engage with those around us.

Better health. There is plenty of research suggesting that reducing stress can lead to improved health. Stress can be the catalyst for autoimmune issues, colds, and even migraines. When we're not trying to multitask constantly or overcommitting our time, we can have more opportunities to breathe deeply, move around, eat better, and play, which decreases the negative effects of hypervigilance, tension, and consistent chemical spikes in our bodies.

Despite these benefits of a simpler schedule, we can still struggle with the *how*. A few of our favorite ways of putting this into practice include:

Learning to say no: Especially for my people pleasers, this is a difficult one to read. But we believe that what's kind and loving for you is *also* what's kind and loving for others. If saying yes means overcommitting, feeling stressed, adding strain, or flat-out leading to exhaustion, you will not be showing up as your best self. And no one needs that. A simple "No, that's not gonna work for me" will usually suffice, but you can also try the "but" trick. As in saying, "No, BUT . . ." Essentially saying no to the original request but offering an alternative that will work for you and is a good compromise.

Prioritizing activities: Time is more limited than money. So, just like we need to prioritize what we spend on, we also need to prioritize how we spend our time. When there are a million things to be doing and only one of you, it's helpful to list it all out and consider each item in order of importance *and* time requirement. Once it's all listed, go back through and number them in order of importance and plan when each item will happen or if it's something that can't happen. This will require accepting that some things on that list will NOT get done. And that's OK. We can allow our abilities and limitations to inform us on what will and won't work for our schedules in this season.

Focusing on one thing: We love to talk about our abilities to multitask, but our brains can truly only focus on one thing at a time. We trick ourselves into thinking we're actively doing many things at once, when really we're just bouncing around, stressing ourselves out and feeling chaotic. Instead, we can use our priorities list to guide us in focusing on tasks one by one. For everything from chores to debt payoff, we will be more likely to go further when we give our time, energy, and attention to one goal at a time.

Routines

You can think about routines as the actions you do regularly. You've got your morning routines, evening routines, before-bed routines, weekend routines, etc. When harnessed and used to our benefit, these consistent activities can allow us to reduce the number of daily decisions we need to make, thereby reducing decision fatigue. Which in turn frees up brain space to make the best decisions with our money and resources. When we've woven tasks into our schedule that benefit our spending, the whole thing feels simpler.

In my (Jill's) work with clients in the mental health field, this is often a go-to category for finding stability. Routines can be implemented quickly and easily and are actions we can make toward our goals and needs. We all love some fast and effective action steps!

Consider the rhythms that are helpful to the life you're cultivating. The patterns you engage in and the ways they can aid your efforts toward "less complicated." Like looking at your income and expenses with each payday and making adjustments as needed. Or negotiating your bills biannually. Or setting financial goals with each new year. Weaving relevant and helpful routines into your already established life can keep a good thing going for the long run.

From there, a great way to simplify routines is to automate! Thanks to technology, we can make singular decisions by using automation to our advantage, cut out decision fatigue and cumbersome tasks, and friggin move on with the rest of our lives. This is an especially important concept to adopt when we begin implementing a plan with our money. From bills to retirement investing, we'll say it again: automate it! Rely less on your memory and availability, and put good money decisions on autopilot.

Simplifying Your Spending

When I (Jill) was a freshman in college, my roommate went to study abroad for a month. With no accountability and only one class, I went a little feral. I was hanging out with friends, playing pranks, and sleeping on floors, and I let dirty clothes pile up so high that I had a hard time opening the door. I would literally crawl over it all, dig to the bed, and fall asleep. At one point I made brownies in the communal kitchen and slid the leftover tray (uncovered) under the door of my room so I could rush off to my next spontaneous activity. It all culminated in an ant infestation. And not just a trail of ants making their way to the brownies, no. I'm talkin' ants covering the floor like a pulsating blanket of insects. I was horrified. Thankfullky, my fast-paced, no-rule lifestyle stopped once both pest control and my roommate showed up. I quickly found an equilibrium that involved renewed hygiene practices and a more rigorous class schedule. I learned the hard way that my nineteen-year-old brain needed structure and accountability.

While I can proudly say that I have never again lived life quite like I did in January 2009, I learned that "winging it" rarely works. Long walks and Sunday drives aside, we usually do best and actually get to where we're going when there's a plan and route to get there. When it comes to spending, it's best to not treat it like lazy afternoons or my college J-term, but instead develop a simple, low-maintenance way of operating.

Creating and following a plan is what makes our money work. Yes, this includes budgeting! It's what will allow you to visually align and prioritize your spending with your values. It provides the guidelines for where you're going and how you will get there. And the best part is: *you* make the rules. You set the parameters. You decide what is manageable.

When you're not staying on top of them, your schedules, accounts, spending, and income can feel unmanageable. And the longer you avoid managing these tasks, the more daunting it can feel. But if you planned simple and beneficial choices up front, the attention your money needs monthly is minimal! It does require a plan, though, which most people call a budget.

If you've ever budgeted before, the word might bring up some uneasy feelings. Budgets are frequent triggers for the deprivation, guilt, and shame cycle we experience when managing money. So, instead, we like to call it a spending plan. For us a spending plan is simply that, a plan for how you want to spend your money in the upcoming month. While budgets elicit feelings of deprivation and restriction, a spending plan is flexible. Your plan allows you to check last month's spending to make sure there were no surprises, helps you to prioritize your purchases, and gives insight on how you need to spend your time and energy to ensure you follow through with your plan. With a spending plan, you're not just focusing on money, you're also looking at the tangibles and intangibles that impact follow-through.

Creating a spending plan is the simplest way to keep track of your progress each month. If you're like Jen, you might prefer to use an app for tracking purchases. Or, if you're like Jill, you may choose to make your own spreadsheet. You can find both of our favorite methods on the resources page for this book at frugalfriendspodcast.com/book.

When you're making a spending plan, you don't need twenty categories, subcategories, and sections for miscellaneous categories. You really just need to know your income and have your list of priorities from chapter 3. Then plan your expenses, savings, and retirement investing around your income.

Your current take-home pay is what sets the parameters of your spending plan. While a lot of people plan their spending around their projected income, we find that planning based on last month's income makes spending a lot simpler. This approach does require building a buffer of cash in your checking account equivalent to about one month's worth of income. We've found that this buffer gives you more freedom when making purchases and eliminates some anxiety about when a bill is being drafted from your account.

When you're planning your current spending, each area doesn't need to be elaborate. For me (still Jill), I have a spending spreadsheet with four columns. The first column is my fixed (and mostly automated) expenses with rows for housing, transportation, bills, subscriptions, phone, and internet. The second column is my discretionary and variable expenses with rows for my spending on food, nonfood, giving, and gas. The third column is for my saving goals with separate rows for my emergency fund and sinking funds. The fourth and final column is my retirement investing. That's it! It's not complex, and for that reason I don't mind looking at it regularly and making adjustments as needed. Here are a few pointers for you to design your own spending plan that works for you:

1. **First,** tackle your expenses: everything you spend money on monthly, both fixed and discretionary. By now you've done a lot of work with your glorious 90-day transaction inventory, and if you haven't already, this is the time to trim and cancel anything unused or unnecessary. After that, put as many bills as possible on autopay. We want to automate *after* trimming expenses so that we're sure everything we want to "set and for-get" is something we value and love buying! Even if you don't love buying electricity, I gotta imagine you value being able to microwave your coffee whenever it gets lukewarm. Thanks to electricity, that's possible. Now that you have a good handle on the expenses you will pay for each month, tally it all up. Find the total cost of your housing, transportation, food, bills, sub-scriptions, entertainment, and anything else you plan to spend on monthly. Keep that number handy.

2. **Second,** look at how much you *want* to spend this month on your current life and how much you *want* to set aside for future needs/goals. This includes discretionary spending, any extra money you want to put toward debt, and amounts you want to contribute to your saving goals. Find the total of all your "hopeful" spending and hold onto that number.

3. **Third,** consider your retirement investment goals. This in-cludes your 401(k) (or comparable plan from your employer), Roth IRA, and/or traditional IRA depending on your situation. Remember that investing is essentially assuring that you can buy what you love for the rest of your life. Keep in mind that the average over-fifty worker expects to retire at sixty-seven, yet the average retirement age for women is sixty-three, meaning many people have to stop working before they plan to. Invest-ing early and often will alleviate stress if your plans for work-ing change. So, with a retirement income goal and date in

mind, write down how much you want to contribute toward retirement investing each month. For example, a thirty-year-old who wants to max out their Roth IRA in 2024 would need to contribute about $583 per month (given the contribution limits for their age and calendar year).

4. **Fourth**, gather all these numbers. If you're a spreadsheet whiz or you're using an app, you should be able to immediately see if your plan has you spending within or over your income. If you don't have a fancy spreadsheet or app, then tally it all up manually and see how the total lines up with your take-home pay each month. Your expenses should theoretically be equal to your income, but inevitably you will have to adjust how much money you put toward each category and which ones need to be trimmed a bit. That said, we all know reality is not going to be perfect, but we can get as close as possible with our plan. When you're creating yours, remember to keep it simple—not every expense needs its own line item. I spend a lot on food, and it's high on my values list, so I just separate my discretionary expenses by "food" and "nonfood." Your 90-day transaction inventory and priorities lists will be your guide to create and simplify your categories.

Spoiler alert: you will need to refine your plan every month and throughout each month! There will be categories you spend more on and others you spend less on from month to month because life never stays the same! How you shift and refine your spending plan is dependent on everything we've discussed already: your values, your season, your future goals, and all the tangible things you do to make better spending decisions.

There have been months where I (Jill) chose to spend less on dining out and entertainment and more on saving for my future emergencies until that category was fully funded (personally that means three months' worth of living expenses stashed away). And other times I spent more on food and bills and less on my sinking funds because we were hosting friends a lot or traveling. Both examples required some sacrifice and intentional decision-making, but both also bought me things I love like peace of mind and quality time with good friends.

Simplifying our space, schedule, routines, and budget are one aspect of curating our external environment. And every decision toward simplification in each of these categories can have a positive effect on our spending. But it doesn't stop here. Our external environment also includes our relationships and how our engagement with others can support all the good work we're doing with our money! That's next.

⚡ Lightning Round ⚡

What in my life feels the most complicated (space, schedule, routines, finances, etc.)? What's one thing I can do to simplify it?

⚠ Action Step

Make a simple spending plan for next month.

CHAPTER 8

Curate Your Community

When Jen and I (Jill) first met, we were both reluctant to hang out. I was on a three-week road trip with Eric in the RV we lived in, and I wasn't exactly interested in collecting new friends while traveling. But Eric, being the extrovert he is and remembering he might know some people in St. Petersburg (one of our stops on our East Coast tour), put out a Facebook post to see if anyone was interested in hanging out. He thought maybe the acquaintances he made years ago while on tour with a band would see it and want to hang. They didn't. But since Jen happened to be Facebook friends with Eric after meeting at a party in San Diego ten years prior but never talking again, his post showed up in her feed.

And when Jen noticed no one responded to Eric's invitation to hang, she felt bad and reached out to offer a group outing at a bar that served free shots at sunset. To be fair, in my memory, it was small glasses of champagne, but Jen always corrects me; it wasn't that bougie.

Our encounter was out of the norm for both of us. I wanted to rest and not spend precious energy "meeting someone I will never talk to again," and Jen wears headphones when she takes her kids to the park to avoid chatting with other parents, so she also isn't the "meet up with strangers at the beach" type. But we took a chance and did something different. As a result, we found something really amazing. We formed a fast friendship and started our own podcast a year later out of the realization that more people could benefit from a friendship like this!

The thing that really connected us? Being able to talk about our debt payoff journeys. Jen was blogging about how she and Travis were working to pay off $78,000 of debt, while Eric and I were choosing nontraditional housing (full-time RV-ing) to put more money toward my student loan debt. Of course, during our St. Pete visit we both enjoyed the free champagne shots, hanging in the hot tub at the KOA where we parked, and catching a free outdoor movie by the water! But more than finding someone who was also interested in having fun without spending a lot of money, I found connection and community.

Jen became a safe place to ask questions about financial terms that previously seemed over my head, and because of her, I started caring about retirement investing. I've come to recognize that learning always happens in relationships. Infants learn from their caregivers, children from their teachers, professionals from their mentors, and in every other human interaction. We learn from each other, not in isolation.

Beyond what our friendship has offered to each other over the years, we have been blown away by the community built around *Frugal Friends*. While the idea of community is embedded in our podcast title, no one could have prepared us for the stories of life-changing moments listeners have experienced as the result of learning alongside us and engaging with each other online. There is true power and wealth to be found in relationships, beyond what can be enjoyed and discovered alone.

I first heard about the term "relational capital," also called "social capital," when interviewing permaculture expert Laura Oldanie on our podcast. We talked about how financial capital, aka money, is only one form of capital we use to acquire things, yet it's all we tend to focus on. When we say capital, we're not referring to superficial or manipulative metrics like "How many friends do you have?," "How many likes and follows are you getting on the gram?," or "How connected is your network?," but rather the depth of connections formed with those in our neighborhoods, online, and among family and friend groups. As we make investments in our relationships and community, we experience increased benefit to all aspects of our lives. This relational capital should be tallied up with all the other forms of capital: material, intellectual, living, experiential, spiritual, cultural, and, finally, our financial capital. When we can value and invest in all of these areas, we will rarely go broke!

Relationships are a vital internal need. When we look at what we value most, the 4 F's (faith, family, friends, and fulfilling work), each one of them is connected to relationships in some capacity. If 2020 and 2021 taught us anything, it's that we can survive long periods of isolation, but we function best in community. Yet sometimes we still avoid it.

People will opt to buy the brand-new lawn mower that sits in their shed most of the month instead of sharing with a neighbor. When an appliance breaks or our clothes lose a button, instead of learning from a friend how to fix it, we pay someone to fix it or buy its replacement. We'll even opt for online shopping over talking with a friend when it's been a rough day. Why is that?

One reason is that our culture highly values independence and self-reliance. Another is because we don't want to be a burden or "owe someone" later. Asking for help is seen as a power shift that we think another person doesn't want or will take advantage of. But these ways of thinking are costing us money, harm to the environment, and lack of connection.

When we can buy ourselves out of our problems, what happens to belonging, sharing, knowing, and supporting?

Imagine with me for a second an existence where you know those around you and you are known by them. You feel like the people around you are helping you become the best version of you and you're helping them do the same. There are shared resources—tangible and intangible, both tools and ideas! But you're not just taking, you're also giving. And every night you sing songs around a fire while holding hands. Just kidding about that last part. But I am trying to paint a picture of the benefits of community, the reciprocity that can happen in relationships, and the ripple effects these benefits can obviously have on all other aspects of our lives. Because curating our relationships is one of the ways we curate our external environment to support values-based spending.

A silver lining for me in the early days of the pandemic was parking our RV on Jen and Travis's property. In February 2020, we parked for what we thought would be six weeks, only to be unintentionally quarantined together for two months. We quickly learned the benefits of shared resources. With nowhere to go and nothing to do, it was a godsend to cook and spend evenings together. We combined what we had on hand, made up for what the other lacked, cooked meals, and enjoyed each other's company every night. Food costs lessened when we shared it, housing costs were offset on both sides, and we didn't miss going out because almost every night turned into a mini dance party.

While I don't think we all need to go live in a commune, we want to emphasize the often-overlooked role community plays in how we spend. And show you how, from book clubs and buy-nothing groups to community gardens and tool libraries, social capital is vital to sustaining a frugal lifestyle.

The Flip Side

Unfortunately, good things still have their detriments.

Water, for instance, is deadly.

It's a by-product of burning rocket fuel.

It's the main ingredient in herbicides and pesticides.

It's the leading cause of drowning.

And 100 percent of people who drink water will die.

Of course, we know these things aren't water's fault, and we still need water to survive. A good, necessary thing can also be not so good, depending on how it's utilized. The same goes for relationships. They're one of our greatest needs, but they can also cause some of our greatest pains.

When it comes to making good, values-based decisions for ourselves and our money, it's worthwhile to acknowledge where relationships can hinder these efforts.

Depending on the community we currently find ourselves in, we could be more prone to spend money we would not otherwise have spent. A study conducted in the UK found that while both individual personality traits *and* environmental cues influence spending decisions, a person's location could predict their spending more accurately than their personality traits.

Meaning you're more likely to spend on the things the people around you are spending money on. We are prone to see what others around us are doing and follow suit, for better or worse. It's every classic Christmas movie of unspoken exterior light competitions building up to eventual fire, and financial ruin. Or it's like that episode of *Bluey* where she complains that her watermelon isn't as red as her friend's and her dad tries to tell her to not be jealous of what other people have when what she has is great. He then immediately sees their neighbor with a new pizza oven and takes the family to the store to buy the exact same one. We can know all the right things to say and do, but we are all prone to the feeling that "the grass is greener on the other side," especially if that side has pizza.

This is also true of the people our friends are connected to. You've probably heard the saying "You're the sum of the five people you spend the most time with," but it goes even further than that. A thirty-year study on smoking found that smoking behavior spreads through not just close friends but also distant social ties, up to three degrees of separation. This shows that we're influenced by our friends' behaviors and the behaviors of their friends. The same went for the people in the study who stopped smoking. The more people around them who stopped, the more likely they would stop. This study ended in 2003, prior to social media, and we're guessing the circle is even wider now. Social media has given us the gift of connection, but it's also given us a lot more people to compare ourselves to.

When you see dozens of people on social media with some new cup, skin-care product, or a cool new pizza oven, you're more likely to also buy it. We want to belong, and we want to know we're making good decisions, often using the metric of "What are other people doing?" None of this is bad, but sometimes it leads to decisions that are not in *our* best interest.

In order to practice values-based spending, we need to acknowledge that we're not practicing it in isolation. The people around us will have a huge impact, both positively and negatively, in how we spend. And there's no one right way to deal with this. The financial responsibility you have for one family member will be different for another. The way you build boundaries with one friend may be different than what it looks like with others. All our relationships are pushing and pulling us in various spending directions, so it's important to realize what our community is comprised of and the ways we can make shifts in each relationship to ensure our spending stays aligned with what we value.

Spending in Community

Before we talk about the nuance of relationships and how they impact our spending, there are three foundational concepts we must take into every relationship:

The first is **understanding ourselves and our values.** It's essentially what this whole book is about. When we have a good grasp on who we are, what's important to us, and the goals we want to achieve, we are less likely to be blindly influenced into spending decisions or lifestyle shifts that aren't for us.

But when we spend based on someone else's values, out of compulsion, obligation, or pressure, we're the ones most impacted. We're left with stuff we don't need or want, lifestyles that aren't fulfilling, trips that incurred debt, brunches with subpar food, and a feeling of defeat that leads us back to thinking "If I had more money, this problem would be solved." As we've said earlier, more money would be great! But if we learned anything from Haley and Justin's muffin moment, we know that if simply "more money" is the metric, then no amount will ever be "enough." Especially when our idea of enough is not tied to intentional actions rooted in personal values. This knowledge of self and what's important to you can't be understated—it's the secret sauce behind an ability to keep scrolling past the IG ad, skip Target's Dollar Spot, and ultimately say easier noes and better yeses around your spending.

You might be thinking, "Yea, yea, yea, *know thyself*, but what if it's not a *me* problem, it's a *them* problem?" You're not alone! This second concept is key, and it involves **establishing boundaries and speaking your needs**. If you struggle with people-pleasing, have a hard time saying no, deal with fears of missing out, or have a pulse, you need boundaries!

In my work as a mental health therapist, boundaries were the number one thing we talked about behind closed doors. Discerning what is and is not OK, identifying needs, taking responsibility for oneself, measuring emotional/mental/relational capacity, and learning how to operate within and out of those realities. Our conversations almost always came back to boundaries. And it's no different with relationships and money!

Barring traumatic situations and abusive relationships, we train people how to treat us. We get to decide what is in bounds and what is out of bounds, and we can respond accordingly. The trouble is societal pressure, cultural expectations, and an innate desire for belonging intersecting with our best-laid plans. We will allow others to take from us or give us things we don't want. Boundaries are the parameters we get to operate within—they define the context for our creativity. And like we said in chapter 3, when given reasonable constraints, we operate better than if everything was a limitless free-for-all.

The last concept is about auditing and maintaining community. It's what I like to call **holding relationships with an open hand**. We can care for ourselves relationally and experience quality community when we allow this very living organism to grow, morph, and shift. It involves tending to our network regularly but giving space for things to change, people to transition, and our own needs to evolve.

When we weave together these concepts of self-understanding, boundaries, and open-handedness with our relationships and spending, we can show up emotionally and financially healthy in our four main groups of relationships.

With Our Families

For those you share a household with, collaboration, negotiation, and a willingness to honor each other's needs, even if you don't fully understand them, is important. Each person brings their own background with money, values, and behaviors to the table, and that mix may or may not be compatible with yours or helpful to your combined financial landscape. Using income and individual values as parameters can be useful for creating spending plans that benefit you both.

When it comes to our long-term partners and spouses, finances are an integral part in the health of those relationships. Power dynamics, roles, lifestyle, methods of communication, patterns of relating, care, and value shown and so much more *all* intersect with money among couples. It's no wonder there are whole books written on finances just for couples!

This category of community plays one of the biggest roles in our day-to-day spending and trajectory of our financial futures. It should be given great attention and care. No person or relationship is perfect, and we'll all find ourselves at odds with our partner eventually, especially on how money gets spent. There are a lot of ways to manage finances as a couple; we have a few recommendations listed on the resources page of this book at frugalfriendspodcast.com/book. We encourage you to find the best method for both of you, despite what other couples around you tell you about how they manage their money.

The most important part about spending money with a partner is to recognize that you don't share identical values. Instead of judging your partner for wanting to spend on things you don't value, encourage them to prioritize what they love and seek to honor their top values as highly as your own. No matter how hard we want our partners to spend how we want them to spend, they usually see it as deprivation. When they see you want them to have what they love most, and more of it, the conversation shifts from "we have to save" to "we want to spend well." And speaking of conversation, we should reframe the questions we ask our partners with the same shifts we used on ourselves from chapter 2. Avoid "why" questions that put people on the defensive and genuinely seek to get curious about your partner's motivations for spending with questions like:

What do you value or enjoy spending money on most?
What's your philosophy on spending and how did you develop it?
What's your perspective on saving and how did you develop it?
What would you like to do with money in the future?
What would you like to see for our financial future?

You may also need to prepare yourself to find a trustworthy counselor to assist in getting on the same page. That in no way means a failure of your relationship. Oftentimes our heated financial conversations and ideologies around money are rooted in something far more intricate and important than what each other chooses to spend on. And we're not always the best at getting to the core on our own.

With kids, they not only cost a significant amount of money, but they also sucker you into buying stuff you weren't planning on buying. Mostly because they're so dang cute. Or you just want to avoid a public tantrum. Jen keeps a "tantrum avoidance" section in her spending plan for times such as these. Either way, the methods of prioritization still apply here. In the situations where adding extra things to the shopping cart or paying for activities every weekend is not an option, look for opportunities to provide for your kids' wants in inexpensive and creative ways. Like buying secondhand toys from

Facebook Marketplace and taking advantage of your local library that offers free local museum passes, video game console rentals, and . . . books!

And know that when it comes to teaching your kids how to spend, it's never too early to start. You can introduce the ideas of values, parameters, prioritization, and caring for your needs at any age. Allowing kids to join in on the process of valuing resources and recognizing not everything is limitless will only benefit them as they grow into conscientious adults. All that said, we still love our radical middle. It's important to create room in the spending plan wherever possible and within reason to buy the things your kid values, whether you value them or not, as you encourage them on their own path of self-discovery and curiosity-practicing.

The rest of our families encompass numerous relationships beyond our immediate household. When it comes to the adult parents, siblings, grandparents, aunts, uncles, and in-laws, things can get dicey. Not everyone will understand or want to respect the boundaries we set for ourselves. But that doesn't need to keep us from defining and adhering to them.

When you encounter pushback on your boundaries, it's important to truly consider what's livable vs. what's not livable—essentially identifying what matters most.

Here's what I mean. Let's say that your mother-in-law expects extravagant birthday presents. The kind that requires the whole sibling group to contribute a few hundred dollars to the pot. There's also a family expectation that it is *nearly* mandatory to attend one or two family trips a year that all require you to use some precious PTO and pay a significant amount toward lodging and flights. Not to mention all. the. junk. you're obligated to take with you after every visit. From your spouse's third-grade picture to the hideous kitchen towels that her friend got on sale at CVS, it's never something you would gladly take home with you. Like food or money.

In our fake scenario, it could be tempting to allow this whole thing to build up to an explosive point where every detail is brought to light and criticized publicly. We all know that would be devastating. Instead, let's say you decide that right now, the biggest strain is the family vacations. So, you say something like, "We want to give you all a heads-up that we will not be attending the family vacation this year. We love you all very much and we value time with you, but this year we are choosing to prioritize other financial goals. We are hopeful to still have meaningful time together throughout the year." You may then suggest a local long weekend away, or regular bimonthly dinners together, or you choose to host Thanksgiving as a peace offering for missing out. Whether it's a straight "no" or a "no, but . . ." you haven't sacrificed your entire relationship and value for your extended family. You've just moved to care for yourself in the way that matters most right now, while continuing to tolerate the pieces that may frustrate you but you can handle. It doesn't mean you can't address more in the future, but it does allow you to pinpoint what's most important and solve for that thing, head-on.

And if just reading that example script brought up feelings of anxiety or discomfort for you, pay attention to those feelings! They are telling you something. It may mean you need to practice communicating boundaries with others on a smaller scale where the stakes are lower, like some of the examples we will give in the next subsections. It may also mean that you need to role-play your own script with trusted people until you feel comfortable with your words before communicating your decisions. We recognize this is no easy task, but the more you advocate for yourself while valuing others, the better off your life and finances will be!

With Our Friends

A lot of impulse spending with friends is the result of not wanting to miss out. Events, concerts, restaurants, activities, and trips are all

FUN! We rarely want to say no to an invite because we both *need* to be around people and we *want* to experience cool things. But we've found separating the mindless spending from the core need can help shed light on what we really want. This gives room for creativity and finding alternatives that may be more conducive for our spending plan.

When you go out to dinner with friends, is it the plated blackened chicken and hummus platter hand-delivered to your table with two rounds of beverages that you value or is it the uninterrupted time spent with the friends catching up? If it's both, can you currently afford both? If not, is there a way you can get creative with how you meet your highest priority value? If you're a foodie and it really is about the food at the restaurant, then eat away! If it's about the friend, offer to host, meet at a park, host a potluck, or enjoy a free event together. We're not saying to never go out to eat with friends. We are saying sometimes we spend in ways that don't actually get us what we truly want. And when our income is not unlimited, we have to sacrifice some things that we love to keep what we love most. Seeking these alternatives also gives room to try new things and learn about others outside the context of our ingrained habits.

Spending within our friendships also has a lot to do with our levels of confidence in what we bring to the table. Recognizing your own worth, uniqueness, and what you have to offer will save you from spending with friends in order to fit in or gain approval. I'm talking to all my girlies who feel the internal pressure to pay someone's way, treat others to lunch, or can't show up without a host gift. Those things are fine, but not when they come from a place of perceived expectations or believing you must spend money because you alone aren't enough. You are valuable apart from what you do for or spend on others. And your generosity can be measured and executed in a way that doesn't put unnecessary strain on your finances. Being generous can also look like giving of your time, a listening ear, and maybe even a gift sourced from home if you don't want to show up somewhere empty-handed. In whatever ways you choose to give, know that it's yours to decide how you want to spend your resources, and this should be done out of desire, not compulsion.

We *can* have the best of both worlds: kindness to our financial selves and cultivated friendships.

Of course, not everyone is going to be on the same page as us or value similar things, and that's okay! We can only be responsible for ourselves, say what works, speak our needs, and invite others in. What our friends choose is not up to us, nor do we know what's best for them. But when it comes to what works for us, we can be clear, kind, and communicative. Whenever possible, we can be the ones making the plans, offering fun free suggestions, and letting our friends in on the financial parameters we've set for ourselves so they can adjust and respond how they want. We can be the change we want to see with the friends we already have.

Take for instance group outings, trips, or events—it's best to set expectations ahead of time and have some transparent conversations *before* any money gets spent. I (Jill) take at least one friend trip a year, and before deciding where we will go, we have a check-in on the total amount of money that everyone is willing to spend. We take the lowest number and work our travel plans accordingly.

For events like bridal or baby showers and bachelorette parties where we are highly involved in the planning and execution, the same principles apply. Whether you're the one in charge of planning or asking questions of the planner, it's uncomfortable at first. But asking all involved something along the lines of "What is everyone comfortable contributing?" Or "I'm able to contribute $50. Beyond the money, are there any other ways I can help with this event?" Being honest about your own capacity will help bring definition to the plans and inevitably decrease anxiety for all! Remember that getting hit with a Venmo request for an absurd amount of money after the celebrations are over is way worse than communicating about costs up front.

And now we're going to share an unpopular, spicy opinion. Brace yourself. It's also possible you choose to limit your participation in an event, even in cases where full participation is expected of you. If up-front communication about money reveals that it's outside of the scope of what's okay for you, kindly decline or offer alternatives. At different seasons of life, there have been times I (Jill) chose not to be a brides-maid or not host an event. There have also been seasons when I gladly spearheaded the baby shower and attended the destination wedding. It's not about being stingy and always saying no, it's about saying a noncompulsory, intentional yes with eyes wide open to what you're agreeing to.

Our true friends, the ones who have our back, do not want us to harm ourselves in efforts of support to them.

With Our Coworkers and Acquaintances

Our friend Sarah works in a really tight-knit dental office that has regular, themed dress-up days. From St. Patrick's Day to Halloween, there's always a reason for wearing themed clothing, hats, and funky glasses. Sarah has described really enjoying the environment she works in but admitted that she spends at least $50 each month buying the matching stuff or bringing in the fun food. Money she would prefer to put toward her debt payoff. Saying no to any of it feels espe-cially difficult because she sees these people every day. And she does actually like them!

The relational expectations with our coworkers and acquaintances may not be high, but the pressure to spend and the demands for our money are still present. From gifts for coworkers' birthdays to happy hours and lunches to kids' fundraisers and those dang Girl Scout Cookies, it's possible to spend a good chunk of change we weren't planning on each month.

Thankfully, you're capable of doing hard things! You can remind yourself of your values and what they mean for your spending. You can check in with the parameters you've set for your money and commu-nicate your chosen action. While it may absolutely mean buying that box of Tagalongs (because that chocolate peanut butter cookie combo is fire), it could also mean opting out of the happy hour, or vice versa. Since this can be a tricky thing to navigate in the moment, let's review some of your options so you feel well-equipped to handle the next request that conflicts with your financial goals.

For the lunch or happy hour invite that is not in your spending plan, remember that "no" is a full sentence. You can choose to opt out. You can catch the next one. You can go and order in a way that makes sense for you. Or you can be the initiator of the plans with suggestions like BYO lunch to the local park (we like this because it doesn't limit others from getting takeout if they want!), coffee walks in the morning before work instead of drinking after, or invitations to free activities. We love city websites and the Facebook events section for finding the cool stuff.

For the pooled gift money that just doesn't make the cut on your priorities list, offer an alternative like being the one to pick up and write the card, order the flowers, or decorate the desk. Your sweat equity and investment of time may be just as valuable as the $20 they were hoping to gather. Depending on your comfort level, you may also choose to share some of the financial choices you are making and why. If you're currently engaging in a no-spend challenge, say it! If you're prioritizing paying off a student loan or credit card and these small decisions are helping you get there, let them know! Oftentimes this is inspirational to others and gives space for them to choose intentional spending.

With Our Internet Friends

Many of us are finding like-minded, helpful individuals and groups digitally. Whether it's a hobby, sport, or area of learning, we get to gather and find connections with others from different parts of the world. There's so much to be celebrated when we are able to find our people both near and far.

But it's not without risk! Even more endless than the friends we can find online is the opportunity to spend. From influencers to scammers, all are vying for a piece of what we've got, and we need to be aware and in charge of our decisions.

Curating the content we engage with offers lots of protection for impulse spending. Choosing to follow the social media accounts that support your current life aspirations and provide the information and learning opportunities you're looking for will serve you better than allowing the algorithm to choose. Recognizing when posts are straight-up ads and when those ads are for products you don't need can keep social media a safe space rather than a spending trap.

This awareness and healthy dose of skepticism is also non-negotiable when it comes to protection from scams. With increasingly sophisticated AI tools, scams are becoming more complex and harder to detect. The misconception that only dumb people get scammed online is just not true. Scammers target smart people in vulnerable seasons of life with scams that are long-term and extremely psychologically manipulative. So, we have to know the signs early to prepare ourselves and protect our finances. Some key things to do and watch out for include:

Don't reply to "wrong number" text messages from unrecognized or blocked phone numbers.

Never download an investing app sent to you from someone who you don't trust for financial advice.

Beware of anyone rushing you to pick up the pace and make your relationship exclusive.

Scammers frequently pose as someone wanting to be romantically involved, but more often they're claiming to just want to be friends. They won't ask you for money; instead they'll show you the money they're making through investments and give you the link to "invest" if you want to. In reality, there are no investments. Other times scammers are posing as banking institutions or a subscription software you use or have used. In these instances, being sure to contact those businesses using your typical methods is advised. Finally, in the situations where scammers are posing as family members from different phone numbers, hang up and call that person directly. Better yet, have a code word with loved ones to confirm legitimacy. All of this will provide protection and keep us from hemorrhaging cash to a crisis that never actually existed.

We don't need to be fearful of the internet, but awareness and intentionality go a long way in providing protection. When we can engage in discerning ways, there is so much benefit and community and so many resources to be found.

But What If I Don't Have the Kind of Friends I Need?

Making friends can be a daunting task. It was so easy in college and even early career life. Practically all we had to do was make a joke within the vicinity of someone our age and suddenly we're sharing chips and queso on the couch swapping insane dating stories.

As we get older, we turn more inward toward family and career, but our need for community never goes away. But because life changes, we never stop needing new friends. Relationships ebb and flow with our seasons, and they will inevitably look different in each decade of our lives. Yet again, the concept of the vital few and useful many remains a trustworthy guide in knowing what we need. We can value our "few" closest relationships and keep them with us throughout life while still benefiting from the "many" relationships that enrich our lives if only for a season.

When previous friendships have fizzled, moved away, or changed in ways that make relating difficult, it's okay to let go. When we let go of a friendship, it doesn't mean the relationship failed or that we're abandoning people, it's simply acknowledging cycles and seasons. Not every person we regularly got together with in one season needs to be the person we are currently getting together with routinely. Things change, people shift, seasons come and go, and sometimes relationships we let go of come back around! It's okay to hold these things with an open hand while also asking, "What can be woven into my life that will be helpful relationally?" Could there be groups and activities that engage you in a cherished hobby or provide mental and emotional care alongside getting you out to meet new people?

When looking to build new friendships, we love Meetup groups for shared interests like reading or crafting, fitness classes, running and cycling groups, faith communities, and volunteer opportunities. They all offer both an outlet for interests and fill in the gaps where we may be lacking relationally. They also give us the opportunity to *be* the kind of friend we want to have. To ask ourselves, "How am I showing up in relationships?" "How are others experiencing me?" "What am I glad to offer in friendships and where can I improve?" Making the small changes that get you closer to the person you want to be toward others is what will create long-lasting friendships where you want them most.

All this self-understanding, boundary setting, and holding loosely allows the organism of community to grow and become a strong place of safety, support, and intentional spending. And we can find ourselves rich in relationships.

When we value others without harming ourselves, we can experience a wealth of goodness within our communities. We can invite and engage others into our values-based spending journey both explicitly and implicitly.

I'm sure glad Jen and I both went out on a limb that one day in April, choosing community even when it didn't feel convenient. That meeting has led to knowledge and support that has absolutely changed the trajectory of my life for the better. Just this one friendship has provided something in a relationship I was previously lacking—safety to chat about financial things—and made space for thousands of others to find their people, feel seen, and be reminded they're not alone in this journey.

Your friends and surrounding community can be your biggest cheerleaders and helpers in living out your values. They can be the ones to join you, encourage you, and remind you of the great things you want to do with your life and money. It starts with you recognizing what those great things are, communicating it, sticking with it, and cultivating that community that makes it all possible.

⚡ Lightning Round ⚡

What would you like to see change in the ways your community impacts your spending?

⚠

Action Step

Find a free event to attend in your area within the next month and invite your partner, a friend, or coworker. OR go by yourself and meet new people.

CHAPTER 9

Contentment Without Complacency

Before Eric and I (Jill) moved into our first RV, we were living in a two-bedroom apartment. While cleanliness and organization have always been important to me, I definitely wasn't minimalist back then. I carried a fondness for the boho chic aesthetic of the early 2000s and loved collecting mismatched odds and ends from yard sales, thrift stores, and consignment shops. If it was free (or inexpensive), it was for me! A common statement from friends when they came over was "There's so much to look at!" I took it as a compliment (it wasn't one) and told them "You're welcome for providing your eyes with entertainment."

I thought I was smart and creative with all the deals I got, treasures I found, and items I repurposed. And I loved the thrill of the hunt, so much so that nearly every weekend I would find myself at a garage sale buying something secondhand. I never spent much money—that was part of the bragging rights—but I also never thought about whether or not I actually needed or wanted more things.

It wasn't until we smushed ourselves into a 300-square-foot home on wheels that I started to connect my collections to my spending habits. I had done the simplifying thing (in a major way), but initially I still went to the secondhand stores because that's what I did for fun on weekends. Even though I'd just purged so many of my belongings, I kept going because it had become a habit. I quickly found it wasn't as enjoyable when I couldn't buy anything. Part of me felt bamboozled into this new lifestyle, and at times I found myself annoyed by the lack of space. But I enjoyed the RV and knew that in order to love the lifestyle, I needed to find contentment with the things I already had and new activities to replace what I previously thought was important to me.

In a world that thrives on discontent, finding contentment is radical. Contentment in its purest form is to feel satisfied with one's possessions, status, or situation. If simplifying and community building are what curates our external environment to create sustainability in our values-based lifestyle, then contentment is how we curate our internal environment (i.e., our mindset). Without contentment, we are susceptible to both the internal and external forces driving us to spend money to solve our problems. With contentment, many of those problems don't exist.

I used to think of the embodiment of contentment as an unhurried elderly woman in her garden. Moving through the shrubs, flowers, vines, and trees planted by her over decades. Taking time to visit each one and tenderly caring, pruning, plucking, admiring. Enjoying the fresh air and giving herself time to close her eyes in the sun.

In reality, there's no way this woman actually exists. Not because there aren't lots of older women in their gardens, but because a person content at all times is impossible to come by. We will never arrive at a place and stay there forever, either literally or metaphorically. Humans are designed to crave, grow, and improve. But we *can* experience peace inside ourselves related to our perceptions of our stuff, our status, and our situation more often than not. Which will ultimately lead to better spending.

The key here is how we choose to *view* our circumstances.

I find it interesting that every aspect of contentment's definition — possession, status, and situation — intersects with our engagement with money. It says nothing about how abundant or luxurious any of the categories are, simply how one "feels" or "shows" satisfaction toward them. Mmm! I could end it there and let us all go ponder that one. But we'll stick together and chat about some of the ways we can experience contentment throughout life and what this means for our money.

Naturally, we can't just talk about contentment without exploring the extremes we could find ourselves in on its spectrum. If contentment is the radical middle, then hustle culture and complacency are on either side. And along the entire spectrum, we can find discontentment. It can crop up as both a restless desire for something you don't have and a dissatisfaction with your stuff, status, and situation. All the opposites of contentment can be found in both extremes.

I have this image of Lizzie McGuire (from the Disney show in 2001 for all my non-Millennials) with a cartoon version of herself on each shoulder. On one shoulder stands her perfect self and on the other shoulder stands her unhinged self. Each version is pleading with the true Lizzie's head in the middle, trying to persuade her to take their advice in the complicated conundrum she found herself in with friends, boys, parents, you name it! The early 2000s loved this specific depiction of our inner monologue and the competing extremes we often need to choose between. In the end, rarely did Lizzie ever fully take either one's advice. Usually it was some combination of the two, mixed with her own creativity.

And here we are, much like Lizzie. On one end we have a hustle culture telling us to work harder, get the job, take the promotion, and start a side business. Hustle, hustle, hustle. On the other end we have another voice steering us toward apathy. Mumbling "What's even the point," whether you work hard or not, there's no such thing as getting ahead. Taxes will happen every year, the debt isn't going anywhere, the house is just gonna get dirty again, and your work will never be valued. Give up. Lean into complacency.

AHH!

True to the sitcom, this is the part where Lizzie screams. I'm screaming a little too.

If I learned anything from Lizzie, it was to take a little from both sides, mix in my own creativity, and find the radical middle. For us, that's contentment without complacency. We don't have to let go of our aspirations and goals, and we're also allowed to take it easy every once in a while. We can train ourselves to take hold of both ends of the spectrum and allow the tension to guide us. We can be pleased with our circumstances without finding ourselves in a place of stagnation or exhaustion.

And finding contentment in the things money both can and can't buy is what gives space to pause and take breaks, while recognizing our responsibility to live into our full capacity.

Of course, contentment is a hard thing to measure or give a five-step guide to achieving. We can't *will* ourselves toward being content. No amount of strong-arming to just "be satisfied" will work. It's such an internalized, deeply rooted perspective that only daily decisions and mindset shifts can develop it. And what makes contentment especially difficult to discern is that it's not bad or shallow to want more and better. Contentment does not require you to suffer in silence, and there is no extra reward in retirement for martyrdom. When our stuff, situation, and status feel subpar, it can be easy to *still* think that more money and nicer things would solve the problem. But we want you to remember, you don't need more, different, or new to be happy.

You Don't Need More, Different, or New to Be Happy

So why is it so dang hard to be content? In a survey conducted by Empower Financial with over two thousand Americans, it was discovered that people in every income bracket thought they needed to earn more money to be happy, with top income earners (those making $250K+) believing they needed an additional $150 to $200K more per year in order to be happy. In contrast, most other brackets believed an increase of $20K to $50K annually would lead to greater happiness.

While there's a lot to dissect there, the thing that stands out to us the most is that no matter where we find ourselves, the propensity to imagine life being better with more will remain. And those with the most still don't think it's enough.

Unmet expectations, past experiences, the people around us, even certain seasons, can give us a distorted perception about what everyone else has and what we should have. Our distorted perception can often lead to jealousy and comparison. These play a strong role in the elusive nature of being satisfied, and they're hard to avoid when we see others around us taking fun vacations, driving newer cars, getting the sweet apartment, renovating their kitchen, or using top tier makeup and skin-care products. These are the times when it feels like our money is what's holding us back from the sweet life. We find ourselves thinking again that just a little more dough, that promotion, that job will give us the edge we need and then we will have enough. But those milestones happen, and our spending rises to meet our earning and we have a new metric for what will be our "enough." Lifestyle inflation is not the enemy, though. When we earn more, it *is* reasonable to spend more. It's when the lifestyle creep is driven by comparison, wanting what others have and going after it solely because they have it and it looks good for them. Only to find it was not enough, did not bring purpose, and was not something we really valued.

Another thing that can derail our efforts toward contentment is when our accomplishments don't feel the way we thought they would.

Even debt payoff, savings, high net worth, and early retirement don't bring joy. We've seen the disillusionment on the other side of these financial milestones when people realize it's not the nirvana they were told it would be. That's not to say we shouldn't pursue these things, just don't expect these things to bring contentment, inner peace, or ultimate happiness. Once we achieve what we've been aiming at for a long time, there's certainly a rush of enthusiasm. It's exhilarating, and we feel unstoppable! But it's not long before we return to our relative baseline of operating and perceiving.

So, what's to be done?! Are we doomed to dissatisfaction? Will we never experience what it's like to have enough? Certainly not!

You can come to a place of satisfaction with what you own and do as well as with who you are and what you've done. You don't have to be a statistic that desires more for the sake of more. Your desires, goals, and actions can be tethered to your values, season, and intentionality. You can feel good about the decisions you make with your time and money. And that feeling doesn't need to be fleeting.

This is values-based spending in action.

But finding satisfaction with your stuff is just the half of it. Finding contentment with who you are and what you've done requires a deeper level of work. Reconciling the various aspects of your personhood and coming to terms with your uniqueness—the parts of yourself that you are proud of and the parts you wish you could change. So many people spend unnecessary money, time, and energy on efforts to alter their situation and circumstances without ever considering what embracing and valuing their current position might look like.

When we are drawn to give more focus to what we don't have versus what we do have, we are bound to experience discontentment. But if we are able to find beauty in our season, appreciation for the journey we've been on, and gratitude for our contributions and experiences, we are more likely to feel at ease and more likely to feel satisfied.

I (Jill) have had times of feeling defeated about the way my life has panned out, especially in terms of finances. The zeal in my twenties for social justice causes but complete lack of value for earning money caught up with me in my thirties. Using only the metric of finances, I was not doing nearly as well as my peers. My social work education and career left me with debt, zero savings, no medical care, and certainly no retirement investment accounts. In many ways, it had me feeling "less than" and even a bit silly for the choices I made in that crucial decade.

While commiserating all this with Jen, it wasn't long before I also recalled the investments I made in myself and in others that are leaving me rich in a way money never will. I've taken part in beautiful, meaningful things over the past fifteen years. From helping at-risk teens graduate high school to supporting marginalized women during crucial times of their recovery to traveling internationally to provide critical care to those experiencing crisis, the people who let me be a part of their journey have provided immeasurably more to me than any amount of money in my checking account. So, while there's not much to show for it in the bank, I can say now that I wouldn't take any of it back.

Every choice we make will have an opportunity cost. There is no world where sacrifice, loss, or disappointment doesn't follow us. I know now that if I had chosen a high-earning career path, there would have been difficulties associated with that too!

So, for you, where are you experiencing dissatisfaction with your stuff, status, or situation? What is within your control? What is outside your control?

In what ways is your degree of satisfaction linked to who and what you're comparing yourself to? Is the standard you use for how well you think you are doing or how great your things are based on your peers? People on the internet? Even your former or previously hoped-for self?

The problem is that nothing is exactly as it seems. There's always a fuller story. You don't know the intricacies of what made "success" possible for that person or the difficulties they may be facing. Instead, focus on what your choices and life experiences produced in you. The lessons you learned and the areas you are most grateful for.

As we move beyond the "what-ifs" of the past, let's imagine what can be done now and moving forward. You have an opportunity *now* to do and become something you can be really proud of in the *next* fifteen years. Starting today, what will future-you be glad you invested your time, energy, and resources into?

Grateful and Growing

We have the freedom to manage our resources in a way that makes sense for us and the ability to spend on the things we love, not just save, save, save. For Jen and me, finding day-to-day satisfaction in our stuff, status, and situation has us leaning into what we're good at. We're also learning, expanding our knowledge and skills, and finding new things we love. And it's these things that have provided longevity in our values-based spending lifestyle, not just a means to an end.

Of course, we're not living in fields of peonies and sugarplums all day. We're not perfect, and our lives are far from perfect. But when we are able to cultivate a mindset of gratitude, we find the long-term effects are contentment and satisfaction.

Gratitude is the practical implementation of contentment, and it's what makes values-based living and spending sustainable.

Here's another *Merriam-Webster* moment: to be grateful is to be "conscious of benefits received." Meaning the things that have already happened or are currently happening. Gratitude does not, and seemingly is not, tied to the future. It's right now.

When cultivating a mindset of gratitude, it's important to focus on two things:

Acknowledging the good things you currently have within your status, situation, and stuff

Identifying the role others play in bringing goodness into your life

Hmm, it's almost as if those simplifying and community building efforts are useful for curating this internal perspective (wink, wink).

To notice the good things and the quality people you have around you, it's going to require looking. When we don't look for things, we don't find them. We can't be conscious of what's bringing us benefit without taking the time to identify it. To do this, it takes practice. A few of our favorite ways to weave gratitude into our day-to-day include:

Journaling Gratitude. This is a five-minute exercise you can choose to do for just two weeks or as an everyday practice. It involves writing down one to five things you are grateful for that day. You can think about questions like: What *do* I have as a result of this current season? In what ways am I experiencing the benefits of the 4 F's (faith, family, friends, fulfilling work). What benefits have I received *today*?

Doing this regularly can help you become more aware about your space, current season, and how you move through life. It gives clearer focus on what's actually important and can even help reset your thoughts. Try it. And take notice of your level of overall satisfaction after a few weeks.

Triggering Gratitude. This one involves the senses and requires moments of slowing down. Similar to the pause we can create before buying something, we can use our senses to trigger a gratitude pause. Like the sun on your face in the morning, the smell of coffee, the voice of someone you love, the feel of something warm; any of it is something to be grateful for in and of itself. Each one can also be the catalyst for listing off even more things you are grateful for about your life and the people around you. You decide what you want your triggers to be and allow each one to be an opportunity for thankfulness.

Sharing Gratitude. You can invite others into your process by sharing with them the good things you are noticing around you. You can also tell them how glad you are for their friendship, love, care, support, whatever it is you receive from them, whether in-person or through a hand-written note. When you include others in your practice of gratitude, it not only solidifies your thoughts further, it encourages you to keep cultivating this grateful mindset. And others receive the benefit of feeling noticed and appreciated.

As you consider all that you have to be grateful for in your present season, also be sure to acknowledge the hard work you've already done to improve your spending and live a rich life beyond the monetary definition. You can celebrate your efforts and successes. All the times you said no to unnecessary stuff, *and* the times you said yes to decisions that others weren't. Your experience is not anyone else's and your unique journey is worth valuing and appreciating.

To revisit my RV story, these exercises were the very things that helped me find contentment and satisfaction in my season. While simplifying felt somewhat forced on me due to space limitations, refraining from spending my weekends at the thrift stores showed me I actually had other interests. I went on more hikes with friends, dabbled in blogging (that one didn't pan out!), and refurbished furniture to sell. When I chose to focus on "benefits received," I realized that I was truly enjoying the lifestyle. I learned to buy quality over quantity and was grateful for my two amazing knives, four dishes, minimal pantry setup (that was actually inspiring me to cook *more*), and a small home we owned outright. I also noticed a positive impact not just on my money but the way I felt about how I managed money. I didn't expect it going into the situation, but gratitude led to contentment, which led to better spending habits and more mindful purchases. It cultivated a way of living and thinking that I still carry with me today despite the 1,500 square feet I live in now.

Now, I don't think you need to go live in a vehicle to learn about what's most important, find contentment, and spend on what you value. That was just my journey. In your own way, seek to find contentment without complacency through a mindset of both gratitude and growth. One that finds satisfaction in the present season but also holds on to and pursues opportunity for more as it aligns with your values. It will require an ongoing process of identifying your "enough" and tethering what that means to your finances. Let's take a look at what we're talking about, specifically as it relates to earning more, paying off debt, and investing.

Beyond Spending

As you practice values-based spending, with your money and your time, we believe a natural by-product will be having more of both.

And an important part of not going broke is knowing what to do with it. We've mentioned throughout the book that spending is only one part of the equation. We wrote this book because we don't think spending gets enough credit for the significance it has in making every other part of the equation easier. But even with that significance, the other parts of the equation can't be ignored. Your income, debt, and investments are equally important. With every intentional spending choice you make, you free up a little more of your time and money to work for you in these areas.

Income

I recently came across a study, separate from the survey we referenced earlier, where every generation (Boomers to Gen Z) named an annual income they thought they needed to be happy. Most generations suggested something between $130K to $190K annually would be sufficient. Except for Millennials. We generation Y-ers cited needing to earn $525,000 annually to be happy.

Now before we all balk at this number and reprimand Millennials for our high debt and unrealistic dreams, the plot thickens.

There's some spicy research emerging here, and even though it sounds like those words shouldn't go together, just trust me. Grab your cup and get ready for this tea.

To answer the question "Do larger incomes make people happier?" two researchers teamed up in an adversarial collaboration. You read that right. Spicy research. Their own independent studies previously led them to different conclusions. You may recall these studies—they're pretty popular. The first found that happiness leveled out around the $60K to $90K mark, while the other study reported a linear relationship between happiness and income with no plateau. These discrepancies in findings led them to join together in an effort to find common ground in the data. What they discovered was that, yes, in most instances more money does make people happier. Literally up until about the $500K mark, there is a positive correlation between people's reported levels of happiness and their annual income.

Okay, Millennials, hitting the nail on the head with your guesses!

But before we get a big head about it, there's an important caveat here. The positive correlation between increased income and increased emotional satisfaction is not true for people who are already unhappy. There are plenty of miserable wealthy people. And unfortunately for them, more money will not solve the problem.

Similarly, for those of us who are not already wealthy, more money will not in and of itself make us happy long-term. But our ability to find contentment, satisfaction, and happiness now, at our current earning levels, *will* follow us into higher-income-earning brackets.

Thanks to this iron-clad science, we don't have to be fearful of making more. If anything, there's a strong encouragement to seek out ways to increase our earning potential. Especially when we can confidently manage our money well, then improving our life, earning more, or spending more is not the enemy. A change in lifestyle or increase of income doesn't automatically mean devastation of contentment. We can aim for something as long as it's informed and we're sure it's actually what *we* want. We don't have to worry about not being able to control ourselves or thinking that mo' money means mo' problems.

What we achieve through our careers won't be our ultimate happiness, but it also doesn't mean achieving more will be our ultimate destruction. You can keep going and be informed as you go. Pursuing contentment along the way. Both when you don't have the high-paying job *and* when you do. Contentment can be found in it all *and* be paired with new, different, and increased goals.

Paying Off Debt

Collectively, households in America have a lot of debt. And Millennials take the cake on having acquired the most debt of anyone. According to the Federal Reserve Bank of New York, in just one quarter, total household debt rose by $212 billion. In that same quarter, credit card balances rose by $50 billion and auto-loan balances rose by $12 billion. Loan delinquency rates also increased across all debt types, except student loans; Nelnet takes no prisoners.

These are big numbers. So huge they almost become unimportant because none of us can really wrap our heads around what billions and trillions of dollars means. But what all this math does tell us is that we're taking on more debt and we're becoming less concerned about paying off that debt. Complacency creep anyone?

Jen and I are truly in the radical middle on debt. Between the two of us we've paid off over $130K of debt and we've both taken out car loans in the years since. We don't think debt is dumb nor do we believe there's good debt. We believe debt is neutral. What we do with our debt and how we view it has so much to do with our current and future financial success. Student loans, car payments, mortgages, small business start-up loans; they can all help us or hurt us. Borrowing is what allows us to go to college when we have time in our twenties, rather than needing to wait until our fifties to afford a bachelor's degree out of pocket. Borrowing is what allows us to get into a safe home while the kids are young, instead of waiting until they're grown to get a roof over their heads. Borrowing is what allowed me to get a vehicle that was safe to drive, instead of the rusting SUV we had with brake lines that went out on us three times in one month. Debt can be a tool. Debt can be debilitating. But ultimately debt is neutral.

For our friend Jamie, this perspective has been a game-changer when it comes to how she thinks and feels about her student loan debt. She graduated from a private university with $87,000 of debt and is still working to pay this off. Even before graduation there were nights she laid awake thinking about the money she was soon to owe. For her, this concept of debt being neutral is what shifted her thoughts about the decisions she made in her education. Whenever she experiences anxiety, or even guilt, about her student loan debt, Jamie works to remind herself that her education was worth investing in. That she is worth investing in. While there are parts of her that wishes she chose a less expensive university, or applied for more scholarships, she's embracing the path she's on and taking reasonable steps to pay down her debt while still living her life. Having a plan in place and following through on that plan is what's helping her tackle the debt, without the debt taking over her life. It's her mindset that has been making the biggest difference in the way she thinks about herself and the permission she has found to still enjoy the things money can't buy (and a few of the things it can!). Jamie's also recognizing that even in debt's neutrality she can experience peace of mind, freedom in spending decisions, greater financial margin to save and invest, and better credit scores for future mindful borrowing if she does pay off her debt. *Especially* high interest debt.

For some of us, debt can feel like an awful chain around our neck when it costs us exponentially more than the amount borrowed due to soaring interest rates. For some of us, it feels like a wealth-building tool.

Contentment doesn't mean complacency with the debt we carry. Contentment encourages us to pay it off in a way that aligns with affording what we love and embracing our season. When people ask us about paying off debt, we emphatically recommend to make paying off any high-interest debt your first priority. That's because working on any other financial goal with high-interest debt is always two steps forward, three steps back. High-interest debt makes everything harder to achieve. What constitutes "high-interest" changes depending on who you ask, but it will typically always include credit cards, personal loans, and private student loans.

Investing

This aspect of finances has been an area I (Jill) have felt the least confident about. And my lack of knowledge and pursuit of other money goals led me to ignore this category of financial literacy. I assumed investing wasn't for me because I was too broke, or too focused on debt-payoff, or too incapable of understanding the intricacies of making my money grow. I had all the excuses. Until I let myself believe that I could have wealth.

It still feels odd saying it. I can have wealth. But for me, I know if I pursue this it means wealth in all aspects of my life. I can experience fullness relationally, emotionally, and financially. And my definition of wealth may be far different from someone else's.

Once we give ourselves permission to pursue growing our money, we start to realize what that could mean for us, our family, and our community. And at that point, it becomes a social responsibility.

This may not come as a surprise, but women are the best investors out there. In an analysis of more than five million Fidelity customers over the last ten years, it was found that on average, women not only saw positive returns on their investments but also outperformed their male counterparts. The bummer about it is that many women don't invest, even if they have the money. That same study reported 31 percent of women had $50K or more sitting in a savings account. Others had even higher amounts they were stashing away, not allowing that money to grow.

Money is power, and we believe power should be in the hands of good, well-intentioned, thoughtful people. Not because good can't be done without money, but it certainly doesn't hurt! It is true that what we do with little we will do with a lot. But what if we can do a lot with our little now, and a lot with our a lot later?

Welcome to investing, my friends. We can own shares of a business, we can earn money from the profits of other companies, we can take part in the stock market. And all of it can yield compounded interest allowing us to retire well, care for our family and friends, and give back to those around us.

This is a personal finance book, not an encyclopedia, so we don't have the space to cover how to invest. There are a lot of great books on that already—we've listed our favorites in the resources page for this book at frugalfriendspodcast.com/book. So, we want to leave you with what we believe to be the most important principles for values-based investing.

When we say investing, we mean for retirement, prioritizing tax-advantaged accounts. "Tax advantaged" accounts just mean you save money on taxes, either in the current year or in the year you withdraw your money from the account. The two types to start with are:

A Roth IRA or traditional IRA, depending on your income level. This can be done through a brokerage like Vanguard, Fidelity, Schwab, etc. IRA stands for individual retirement account, meaning you can open one on your own—you don't need your employer or a financial advisor for it.

A 401(k), 403(b), 457(b), or other employer-sponsored plan. This account can be Roth or traditional just like an IRA, but you can only get it through your employer. Meaning you don't have control over where it's at, what it costs, and possibly even what your money is invested in. While 92 percent of state and local government employees have access to a retirement plan, only 69 percent of private industry employees have access. If you are fortunate enough to have one, always take your employer's match. A match is not "free money," it's part of your compensation package that you can choose to refuse. If you're self-employed, there are options, like a solo 401(k).

To wrap up our conversation on investing, we'll mention one of the vital few ways to save money that we didn't talk about in chapter 6: investment fees. The average fee for a financial advisor is over 1 percent of assets under their management, i.e., your money. Which doesn't seem like a lot until you get to $100,000 invested. By that point, you'll be paying about $84 per month to have your money sit with this advisor. That's in addition to any other fees associated with putting money in or taking money out. You're not just losing money to fees but missing out on the compound interest that money could be making you. According to a 2023 report by the Securities and

Exchange Commission, over the course of twenty years, a 1 percent annual fee can reduce the value of your portfolio by about $30,000. And that's a very conservative number. Many sources report the number to be closer to $60,000.

We have the internet to thank for the ease of overspending, but it's also made investing easier and much more affordable. And there are very few spending decisions that will save you $30,000 as easily as managing your own IRA.

Don't Go Broke

If contentment is the radical middle, the ideal marriage between the two extremes, then it's not asking us to abandon aspirations or desire for more. It's also not asking us to ignore the need to rest, pause, and do nothing. Instead, it's taking the good and beautiful on both sides while appreciating the "benefits received" right in front of us.

In every facet of your finances, you can be borrowing from both ends of the spectrum and finding the third option. The solution offered by your "perfect self" on one shoulder and your "unhinged self" on your other shoulder mixed with your own creativity. You can "Lizzie McGuire" this thing, making decisions that work for you as you aim at contentment and financial growth.

When you master your spending, find your enough, and achieve financial goals, you set yourself up for a more content and satisfied outlook. You are also more equipped to make informed and insightful decisions about your stuff, status, and situation.

Just don't fall into the trap of believing you value everything or succumbing to the pressure of achieving all the things, all at once. Also, don't give up! Keep moving forward toward the life you want and the person you want to become, even if you need to take breaks or stretch the timeline a bit. Honor your season, embrace simplicity, lean into your community, invest in the things that matter most, find the radical middle, and look for small ways to immediately enjoy the things money can't buy.

⚡ **Lightning Round** ⚡

In what area do you feel the most discontent (stuff, status, situation)? What is fueling the lack of satisfaction?

⚠ **Action Step**

Take five minutes to write down what you're grateful for about your life and experiences (acknowledge benefits received). Bonus: Open a Roth IRA if you don't already have one.

CHAPTER 10

Big Impact Energy

My dad quit smoking when I (Jen) was nine. I remember my age because it was halfway to adulthood, eighteen, and I was convinced that if he smoked past my ninth birthday, I'd become so accustomed to it that I would start smoking too. My logic has always erred on the side of pessimism. But he must've taken me seriously because just before my ninth birthday he took me out back, handed me his last pack of cigarettes, and told me to break them in half. The pack was about half full, but I remember I had to do several at a time because I couldn't get all of them. With each break, light brown flaky Marlboro bits burst open like confetti until they were all broken, lying in a pile at the bottom of a trash can with no bag in it.

My dad never picked up another cigarette. His cold turkey quit wasn't surprising. He was a recovering alcoholic who quit drinking cold turkey when my mom refused his marriage proposal until he got sober. And there was never a drop of alcohol in our house or at any of our social gatherings my entire youth. I don't know if cigarettes were how he gave up drinking, but I do know he replaced his cigarettes with Popsicles. From that day on we could never have enough Popsicles in the house. As a construction worker, I don't think he had access to them at work, so when he got home there was almost always one in his hand. When the Popsicles showed up on his waistline, he got a stationary bike and would wake up at 5 a.m. every morning to spend an hour on the bike.

He died of cirrhosis when I was sixteen, even after twenty years of sobriety. The undiagnosed hepatitis C had progressed too far to treat. While he knew how much I loved him, at sixteen I didn't know how proud of him I should've been. To overcome the addictions he had to drugs, alcohol, and cigarettes was remarkable enough. And then to replace them with healthy habits like exercise was something no one told him to do, no one around him was doing it, he just did it. When he got too sick to cycle, he'd still wake up every morning at 5 a.m. and write fun little notes to me and my mom. He made it all look natural.

Today, when I think of him, the first thing I think about isn't the family vacations or things we did. I think of lying in bed hearing the whir of the stationary bike in the front room. I think of his character that was consistent and kind whether privately at home or out in public with acquaintances or friends. He was the barometer by which I measured what I was capable of, and he gave me the unspoken permission I needed to believe I'm capable of anything. But it didn't happen immediately.

There have been times in my life I've wanted to change something, but I didn't want to change too drastically from the people around me. I didn't want people to think I was too big for my britches, that I was trying too hard, and I definitely didn't want them to admire or think too highly of me. I was hesitant to look for a community that did things differently, because where would I find them? That was scary, you never know what you're gonna get, and I didn't want to hurt my current friends' feelings. I wanted to fit in more than I wanted to improve. It took years after my dad's passing to realize what he had done. To realize what he risked by doing things differently and how what he gained was so worth it. And it gave me permission to make changes in my life, better late than never.

We all have someone in our lives who has given us permission: to believe something, do something, or become something greater than we believe for ourselves. Not explicit approval, but a silent signal that it's okay, to come on in, the water's fine. Whenever my dad wanted to do something, he did it. Whether it was quit smoking, lose weight, or whatever, he was not the man to sit around and complain. His first instinct was to take action. If you know me personally, you know I take the same approach to life now, whether it's starting a blog, recording a podcast, or writing a book. In fact, this book might never have happened without someone's permission.

I'd always wanted to walk into a bookstore and see my name on a book, but I didn't think our platform was big enough. When I shared my dream with my friend John, who'd recently published a book, he told me my ideas were good enough and that I wouldn't know for sure unless I tried. Turns out he was right.

Today we want to give you permission.

We don't know what your situation is, but we hope we showed you in this book how adaptable improving your spending habits can be. That wherever you are, you can do something, and you can start today. You don't have to start with waking up at 5 a.m. or getting a stationary bike! Maybe your next step is just getting curious about what you truly value. Maybe it's reevaluating what you thought you valued, or maybe it's finally time to pull the trigger on selling a car or something else with a payment that's too high. The great thing is that you don't have to follow every suggestion in this book to be successful.

As you find permission to make the changes and do the out of the ordinary with your spending, you also help others find their own permission. Changing the way you spend gives the opportunity to impact hundreds of lives: your family, friends, coworkers, strangers on the internet, and people across the globe who you will never meet. No influencer status needed.

Permission Givers

It has long been said that consumption drives the economy. The foundation of modern macroeconomics tells us that demand drives supply, that healthy economies spend or invest more than they save, and that governments should always seek to increase spending, even if it means going into debt. For the last one hundred years, it has been our civic duty to consume. And consume we have.

In 2023, the average American made $150 worth of impulse purchases every month. The year prior, before rampant inflation settled in, that amount was over $300 on impulse purchases every month. So, when inflation cools and your lifestyle inflates, what if your impulse spending didn't? What if it stayed at $150 per month instead of inflating back to $300? That's $150 per month, $1,800 per year that you can put toward things you really love. After five years, you'll have preserved $9,000. And along the way, if you gave permission to five friends who saved a cumulative $45,000, and they each gave permission to five more friends who saved a cumulative $225,000, who gave permission to five more friends, you would have a ripple effect that led to $1.12 million that stayed in the hands of 125 of your friends and out of the hands of shareholder-friendly, impulse marketing savvy, big businesses. Just by implementing the information in this book to help you avoid impulse buying a handful of items at the grocery store, some clothes from Amazon, and a few well-intentioned but unused planners, you have the potential to put millions of dollars back in the hands of those who will do the most good with it. Because we know who will not do the most good with it.

After nonfinancial corporate profits reached an all-time high of $2.09 trillion in 2022, economist Paul Donovan published a note on "profit margin-led inflation," describing how companies, particularly retailers of food and consumer goods, convinced people that they needed to raise prices because of inflation and labor shortages when they actually didn't, and no one questioned it. The perfect storm allowed businesses to raise prices more than what was needed with no loss in consumption, leading to soaring profit margins. And no one would admit that those companies were driving more of the inflation than they were responding to.

But this perfect storm was driven by our consumption. Spending in 2023 increased even after adjusting for inflation. And this doesn't take into consideration the long-term costs associated with our purchases.

Global consumption of fast fashion has increased by 400 percent in the last twenty years and 85 percent of textiles end up in landfills. Every year 30 to 40 percent of all food produced for human consumption in America ends up in landfills. That's more than one hundred billion pounds, worth more than $400 billion. Grocery stores are responsible for only $5.6 billion of that. The average American consumer is responsible for most, spending an estimated $1,300 per year on food that ends up being thrown away. This doesn't just impact our grocery bill directly, it also increases our taxes and utility bills. A total of 10 percent of the US energy budget is spent transporting food, and our taxes subsidize a large portion of US food production, of which a third is wasted. This waste leads to the need for more landfills, which can cost cities up to $43.5 million a year in dumping fees. A leading reason why the garbage industry has been more profitable than the stock market since 2015.

We're also incentivizing businesses to look the other way when faced with human rights violations in manufacturing. They lower their responsible sourcing standards to keep pace with our demand. Everything from the clothes you wear to the car you drive has been linked to forced labor at some point in the manufacturing process.

Our overconsumption gives permission to businesses to engage in these unethical business practices. Our willful silence as we continue to "buy now" tells them we want them to keep doing what they're doing.

Values-based spending is about so much more than getting what you love. It's also your responsibility to the world around you. It's your civic duty to buy what you love and not consume beyond it. Your spending is how you advocate for yourself, your friends, family, community, and people you will never meet who may not currently have the resources to advocate for themselves. Because if we don't, the problem will get worse.

And here's the thing: Our responsibility to do better for others can be a heavy burden. We all know we should be concerned about helping the environment, but there are so many things going "wrong" and so many "right" things to do that we may get overwhelmed. It's the same with responsible spending. There's no way to know how every business is sourcing their goods, manufacturing their products, or treating their workers. It's impossible, and it leads to giving up on doing anything. But every small effort in the right direction makes an impact. A big impact.

We can tackle large problems by taking small steps. One example is with our cell phones. According to the International Energy Agency, manufacturing in China emitted 11.9 billion tons of carbon dioxide emissions in 2021, accounting for 33 percent of the global total emissions. In 2022, over 40 percent of US goods were imported from China, with electronics at the top of the list. Most people upgrade their phones every two to three years. One small step anyone can take is keeping your current phone for one more year than you may have planned on. If everyone did it, we could cut new production by 1.39 billion phones in less than five years! It probably won't happen, but we can dream, right?

Where the big impact is really possible is through these small changes. On an individual level, if you kept your phone for three years instead of two, you'd personally buy four to five fewer phones over thirty years, which doesn't seem like a huge impact, but it could save you at least $4,000. But you also give permission to others to keep their phone for an extra year. The more normal it becomes to wait that additional year, the more people who'll do it, including some of the 12 percent of Americans who upgrade their phone annually. That's around $15,000 per customer those companies miss out on over thirty years. We're usually so focused on wanting to make big individual changes that we forget how powerful small collective changes are in the long-term. And when more people adopt these small changes, the marketing narrative shifts away from "newphoria" to a demand for higher quality and sustainability, not just in technology but across the board. Only when the money leaves do companies have an incentive to go find it.

In business, money is the only thing that talks. We know individuals with the most money have the loudest voice, but collectively we can speak just as loud. We saw this firsthand after several price hikes in 2023 led to a slowdown in sales and ultimately forced companies like Target, Pepsi, and Walmart to lower prices on their products. Restraint from consumers shifted the practices of large corporations. And while most companies won't lower their prices, money talks. And the more intentionally we spend our money, the louder we say what we will and will not tolerate.

Beyond the Money

Values-based spending will require shifting your lifestyle in ways you hadn't expected, toward the things you love. Whether it's more time with family made possible by simplifying or finding a new hobby as the result of your curiosity practices, or changes you make in your housing and transportation purchases that give room for a great vacation or even debt freedom! Whatever it is you love, putting your resources toward that will be worth it, but it won't come without discomfort. Your habits will change, relationships will change, schedules and routines will change. There will be a lot of friction in the process of altering your direction. Embrace it. Value it.

Last year we recorded an episode with Nicole Johnsey Burke of Gardenary Co. about growing a garden with whatever space you have. I (Jen) was not super-interested in the episode at first because I had no desire to garden. Jill is the gardener. I do not have a natural green thumb, nor do I have the desire to maintain a garden when I can buy my produce so easily and affordably from the grocery store. Before we started recording, I told her "This one's for Jill, I don't garden, I cannot keep anything green alive." In response, she asked me, "What are some of the current challenges we all face in life?" We started nam-ing them. We're busy, stressed, tired, lacking connection. Challenges I didn't think had anything to do with gardening. But she went through every challenge we listed off and explained how gardening solved for each one. How being outside reduces cortisol levels, thereby decreas-ing stress, the ways sunshine increases our energy levels and enhances our mood, and that this simple way of producing veggies at home in-vites neighbors, kids, and friends into the yard to participate, giving us some much-needed human connection. By the end of the interview, I was picturing myself in my garden, resting in something I'd cared for with my own hands, physically reconnecting with the earth, spending meaningful time with my sons as they witnessed seeds transform and learn how food grows, and eating nutritious food that came from my backyard.

Nicole went on to explain that for most people who don't garden yet, they'll say it's because they don't have a green thumb, don't have enough space, not enough sun, not enough time, not enough money, whatever. But what it really boils down to is that they just don't see the value in it. Why put in all the hard work, fight the bugs and plant rot, just to have a mediocre zucchini that you could've bought at the grocery store for far less effort, assuming you'd even have chosen to buy zucchini at all? *It's impossible to stick with it if you don't find enough value in the practice to dedicate yourself to learning the skill.* Instead, Nicole invited me to practice gardening not for what it could produce for me but for how it could serve my internal needs.

In his book *Drive*, Daniel Pink looks at studies done at MIT and other universities about what motivates us to do things. He found that external rewards like money or the avoidance of punishment only re-sulted in better performance in basic tasks, such as getting yourself a little treat for getting through the day or doing the dishes to avoid ticking off your roommate. The studies found that if the task involved cognitive skills like decision-making, innovation, and creativity, internal motivators were far more effective than external. Internal motivation means that your motivation to accomplish something comes from within you. There's no treat or punishment driving you, you simply want to do it.

Values-based spending, like gardening, isn't a basic task. It's a creative act full of decision-making, innovation, and creativity. And if you want to master it, you have to be internally motivated to do it. You have to value not just what it can do for you but how it serves you and the people you care about.

Think about why you started this book. You may have wanted to save money so you can pay off debt or catch up on retirement. Maybe you wanted to be able to stick to a budget that, on paper or app, should be doable. Or because you don't care about getting rich, you just want to enjoy your life without going broke. You keep reading stories on the internet and social media about people who've achieved the goals you want and live the life you're striving for. But somehow the knowledge that it's possible is never enough to keep you going.

Being inspired by others' stories is beautiful, but it's external motivation. It won't give you the internal motivation required to make difficult changes. Believe the difficult changes are worth making. Believe in it enough to devote the time it takes to fall in love with the journey. Because when you love the journey in all its successes, frustrations, benefits, challenges, and impact, then you stop thinking of values-based spending as a means to an end and start embracing it as the journey to getting what you love most. Also like gardening, spending is a skill, and you can learn that skill and get better and better at it over time.

Your Turn

Life is about more than money, but money touches everything in life that's important to us. That's why every positive change you make with your spending directly correlates with getting more out of life. The concepts you've learned in this book will eventually transcend spending money and help you spend all your resources better. And before you know it, you'll be frugal.

We started the book acknowledging that frugality is not typically seen as a fun lifestyle. It brings up pictures of a childhood full of frumpy hand-me-downs, dads yelling about the thermostat, and grandmas rinsing plastic bags. Very eco-friendly but not very fun. And yes, when taken to extremes, it's pretty boring. But in its purest form, it is the solution to the challenges most important to us. And we are obsessed with it.

To us, frugality isn't just about spending money well, it's about spending all your resources well: money, time, physical space, natural resources, mental energy, etc. Values-based spending is how we decide to steward our limited resources to make sure we're getting the most out of them. We are whole people, and money isn't always the most important thing to us at any given time. But with values-based spending, managing money well is a smaller part of a bigger overarching purpose.

When you take action on what you've learned in this book, you are giving yourself permission to make changes in your finances and beyond. When you live and spend in alignment with what you love, you also let the people around you know that they too can buy what they love. You lead your children by example, you encourage your partner to pursue their values, you give friends and coworkers permission to say yes and no, and you help your family break generational biases about money.

You vote with your money, not just by punching a ballot card in a rec center once a year, but every day with every dollar. And you find value not just in what values-based spending can do for you but how it serves you. You know that every spending choice you make has an impact, whether immediate or eternal.

Contrary to popular belief, our brains are not "hardwired" to keep consuming more and more. Yes, our culture values what you have and how you look—this book is not going to change that—but you can change. Seriously, the brain has an incredible amount of plasticity. You can retrain your brain at any age.

You won't be one to get inspired quickly but fall off because of the surprises life inevitably brings. You can change your life, the lives of people around you, and of those you'll never meet with whatever income you have. But it doesn't happen overnight. It takes time to afford the dream vacation, pay off debt, improve your salary, and invest for retirement. And that's OK, that's how it's supposed to be! Reality is boring and steady and won't go the way we expect it to. If you get to know people who are consistently achieving their goals, you'll start to realize that there's nothing special about them that uniquely positions them to succeed. It's their commitment to the process. They value why they're working toward something as much as what they get from doing it. They eventually fall in love with the daily practice as much as, if not more than, the destination. In fact, when you focus so intensely on the destination, you miss opportunities throughout the process to achieve successes you didn't know were possible. We chase goals so tirelessly we forget to check along the way to make sure they're still the right goals for us.

Whatever your reason is for values-based spending, don't idolize the end result, fall in love with the journey. Don't put the destination on a pedestal—it doesn't belong there—and it won't earn the honor you're giving it.

If you want to make big changes, they come over time. We know you can do it. Not in the "If we can do it so can you" sort of way. But in the "You can get better at any skill you give your focus to" kind of way. You can define what you love, say no to what you don't, and don't go broke in the process.

Acknowledgments

Our Collective Gratitude

Thank you to our Frugal Friends Community for widening our circle of listeners beyond Jill's mom and helping us understand the true value of relationships; what can be discovered, refined, and achieved when we invite each other in. This book represents our collective ideas, and it's our love letter back to you.

To Goldie Gumban, our manager of everything. If it was your face we could put on this cover just to show our appreciation, we probably would have! We're still not sure quite where you came from, but we *are* glad you've stuck around. From keeping the Frugal Friends business afloat while we disappeared to write this thing, to helping us in the final hours to cite our sources, you're the MVP and we could sing your praises for dayz.

To our triple threat, behind-the-scenes dream team: our agent, Heather Jackson, who took a chance on us, believed in this book, and guided us expertly through the world of traditional publishing. Our editor, Emma Effinger, who has understood our message from the start and has been a consistent, calm encourager toward the finish line. And our copyeditor, Leda Scheintaub, for tightening this thing up and making our voices sound better than they ever did on the podcast.

To Paige Pritchard, Allison Baggerly, Haley Brown-Woods, and Joshua Becker—your insight, expertise, and experience shared in these pages are what completed this book. People will understand what we're trying to say now because you all said it best and you chose to say it here.

To Wendy Norman for answering our frenzied, last-minute request for author photos. You made us laugh, and you made us look good.

To Jesus, for being bigger than the idol of consumerism.

Jen's Gratitude

To Travis, for being the catalyst that started this whole journey for me. I was fine on my own, but my life has exponentially increased because of you. You are the best partner, best dad, best handyman, and worst schedule keeper I could've ever been blessed with. Thank you for your patience with me, your belief in me, and your love. There is no one else I'd ever want to do life with.

To my boys, Kairos and Atlas, when you learn to read, I hope you read this book and know that you are my highest value and purpose in life.

To my mom, thank you for being there whenever I've ever needed you. You have always been a safe space, and I don't take that for granted.

To Jill, thank you for taking this ride with me. I still don't know why you'd want to do a personal finance podcast! There's no one else I'd want to, or probably be able to, work this closely with. I'm so grateful for what we've built professionally, but I'm leaps and bounds more grateful for your friendship. I'm glad we've made it legally binding.

To Lisa Rowan, thank you for being my mentor through the years. For reading everything important I've ever written and making it ten times better. For refusing to ghostwrite this book when I asked you to. For believing in this book even before I did. Thank you for taking the time to read it at maybe one of the busiest times of your life. I would not have felt as confident about sending it in without your eyes on it.

To Caroline Vencil, thank you for your fierce support over the years. To Joe Saul-Sehy, thank you for believing in our podcast and this project. To John Stange, thank you for speaking the words I needed to hear that started this whole journey.

To the women who have shaped me in big and small ways over the last twenty years: Georginia Schutte, Katie Barnes, Alyssa Aviles, Jessica McMahan, Katie Thomas, Kayla Higginbotham, and Shelley Hancock.

Jill's Gratitude

To Eric, for being the best human I know. Your reckless support of my ambitions and steadfast, calm, loving presence when those ambitions feel like a dumpster fire is why I'm still standing. Thank you for being the mastermind and biggest supporter behind this whole thing. And for building our house, starting our podcast, writing our music, fixing our audio (and other) problems, and making dreams come true. You're phenomenal at everything you do, and you make life good.

To my momma, for your limitless love and support always. You consistently know what's needed, from tea *with* honey to pH test strips in the mail; you always take good care of me. Thank you for giving me the experiences I needed to write this book and for teaching me how to enjoy the simple pleasures of life regardless of finances.

To Gimba, for your deep love and care. For instilling the value of a good wooden spoon, introducing me to the glorious world of thrifting, and for always asking if I'm behaving. It's really the only reason this book is devoid of cursing.

To Dad, for your love and encouragement and for teaching me that everything is negotiable; it really came in handy during this book deal.

To Mom and Dad Sirianni, for your love and for cheering me on. From the food you cooked to the appliances you fixed, and all the awkward pictures you took of Jen and me writing—you made the labor of becoming an author far more manageable.

To my older sister, Jessica McCann, whose approval always mattered most. Thank you for never withholding your encouragement and belief in me. I love you dearly and am so glad I have you.

To my younger brother, Andrew Littrell, you really should read this book. And you should know how fond I am of you. I love you deeply, Bubba.

To my nieces and nephews (Dean, Lydia, Baet, Jack, Amelia, and Auggie), my heart grew with love at each of your births. Thank you for teaching me more about how to find what I value and giving me the best, most playful brain breaks in the writing process.

To Bethann Miller, for being my biggest fan and letting me be yours. Your wisdom and humor are unparalleled, and I'm a grateful recipient of both. What I've learned from you shows up a lot in these pages, and I'm forever glad to call you friend.

To Jen, you're the champagne I wanted and the shot I needed. It's your brilliance and friendship that keep me around. Thanks for feeling sorry for us in 2018 and for saying you'd never start a podcast. Your "never"s are the best of what we've created together.

Finally, to all my ladies both near and far who know the intricacies of what life has looked like surrounding this book. For the unending support you offered and all my shenanigans you've put up with: Jenna Ball, Ashlyn Bergey, Sharon Mangum, Lianna Kemmerer, Brittany Wrigley, Chelsea Saurman, Brittany Rizzo, Brenna Henricks, Kate Saurman, Sam Kautz, and Jacqueline Mulder. Your friendships are what strengthens me. That and all the hot dogs and margaritas.

Notes

Introduction

3 a $700 per month cost of living increase in the last two years: Matt Egan, "US Inflation Means Families Are Spending $709 More Per Month Than Two Years Ago," CNN, August 11, 2023, https://edition.cnn.com/2023/08/11/economy/inflation-rate-spending/index.html.

Chapter 1: What Is Love?

21 In a 2024 Gallup poll: Dan Witters, "U.S. Depression Rates Reach New Highs," Gallup.com, May 17, 2023, https://news.gallup.com/poll/505745/depression-rates-reach-new-highs.aspx.

21 rate of anxiety among eighteen- to twenty-five-year-olds nearly doubled from 2008 to 2018: Renee D. Goodwin et al., "Trends in Anxiety among Adults in the United States, 2008–2018: Rapid Increases among Young Adults," *National Library of Medicine*, August 2020, https://www.ncbi.nlm.nih.gov/pmc/articles/PMC7441973/.

24 Like in a Pew Research study: Patrick van Kessel, et al, "Where Americans Find Meaning in Life," *Pew Research Center*, November 20, 2018, https://www.pewresearch.org/religion/2018/11/20/where-americans-find-meaning-in-life/.

25 69 percent of Americans have three or more close friends: Isabel Goddard, "What Does Friendship Look Like in America?," Pew Research Center, October 12, 2023, https://www.pewresearch.org/short-reads/2023/10/12/what-does-friendship-look-like-in-america/.

26 strong associations with psychological health and well-being: Summer Allen, PhD, "The Science of Generosity," Greater Good Science Center, May 2018, https://ggsc.berkeley.edu/images/uploads/GGSC-JTF_White_Paper-Generosity-FINAL.pdf.

30 liposuction and gastric bypass surgery outpaces inflation: Jannik Lindner, "The Most Surprising Weight Loss Industry Statistics and Trends in 2024," GITNUX, accessed December 16, 2023, https://gitnux.org/weight-loss-industry-statistics/.

30 Ozempic, known generically as semaglutide, was Science.org's 2023
    Breakthrough Drug of the Year: Jennifer Couzin-Frankel, "Science's
    2023 Breakthrough of the Year," *Science*, December 14, 2023, https://www
    .science.org/content/article/breakthrough-of-the-year-2023.

Chapter 3: Can't Buy Me Love

62 *Harvard Business Review*: Oguz A. Acar, Murat Tarakci, and Daan van
    Knippenberg, "Why Constraints Are Good for Innovation," *Harvard Busi-
    ness Review*, November 22, 2019, https://hbr.org/2019/11/why-constraints
    -are-good-for-innovation.

Chapter 4: Manufactured Desire

71 The U.S. Bureau of Labor Statistics reported: Elaine Chao, "100 Years
    of U.S. Consumer Spending Data for the Nation, New York City, and
    Boston," U.S. Bureau of Labor Statistics, May 2006, https://www.bls.gov
    /opub/100-years-of-u-s-consumer-spending.pdf.

73 buying all this new stuff is contributing to 60 percent of all greenhouse
    gas emissions: Diana Ivanova et al., "Environmental Impact Assessment of
    Household Consumption," *Journal of Industrial Ecology* 20, no. 3 (Decem-
    ber 18, 2015): 526–36, https://doi.org/10.1111/jiec.12371.

73 Neuroscientist Robert Sapolsky trained monkeys: Susan Weinschenk,
    PhD, "Shopping, Dopamine, and Anticipation," *Psychology Today*, Octo-
    ber 22, 2015, https://www.psychologytoday.com/us/blog/brain-wise/201510
    /shopping-dopamine-and-anticipation.

75 begins reversing within just two weeks of abstinence: Thomas Wobrock,
    MD, et al., "Effects of Abstinence on Brain Morphology in Alcoholism,"
    National Center for Biotechnology Information, January 22, 2009, https://
    www.ncbi.nlm.nih.gov/pmc/articles/PMC3085767/.

75 77 percent of athletes with mild traumatic brain injuries recover within
    four weeks: Stephen Kara et al., "Less Than Half of Patients Recover Within
    2 Weeks of Injury after a Sports-Related Mild Traumatic Brain Injury: A
    2-Year Prospective Study," *Clinical Journal of Sport Medicine* 30, no. 2
    (March 2020): 96–101, https://doi.org/10.1097/jsm.0000000000000811.

77 the first paperless cockpit: Gary Keller, "294. How ONE FedEx Leader
    Used the ONE Thing to Achieve Extraordinary Results, with Bob Minford,
    VP Airline Technology," *The ONE Thing Podcast*, Episode 294, April 12,
    2021, https://the1thing.com/captivate-podcast/294/.

82 Steve Jobs once said: Edward Capaldi, "Focusing Is about Saying No,
    Steve Jobs," YouTube, accessed August 29, 2023, https://www.youtube.com
    /watch?v=JbEjAFrvJv0.

Chapter 5: Why We Impulse Shop

93 **American Psychological Association found:** Sophie Bethune, "Stress in America 2023," *American Psychological Association*, November 2023, https://www.apa.org/news/press/releases/stress/2023/collective-trauma-recovery.

94 **In a study:** Zhihua Luo et al., "Treadmill Exercise Modulates the Medial Prefrontal-amygdala Neural Circuit to Improve the Resilience Against Chronic Restraint Stress," *Communications Biology* 6, no. 1 (June 9, 2023), https://doi.org/10.1038/s42003-023-05003-w.

94 **plenty of research:** "Meditation: A Simple, Fast Way to Reduce Stress," Mayo Clinic, December 14, 2023, https://www.mayoclinic.org/tests-procedures/meditation/in-depth/meditation/art-20045858.

98 **RetailMeNot found:** RetailMeNot, Inc., "RetailMeNot Survey: Deals and Promotional Offers Drive Incremental Purchases Online, Especially Among Millennial Buyers," RetailMeNot, Inc., April 25, 2018, https://www.prnewswire.com/news-releases/retailmenot-survey-deals-and-promotional-offers-drive-incremental-purchases-online-especially-among-millennial-buyers-300635775.html.

98 **Customers hated it:** Brittain Ladd, "Ron Johnson Killed J.C. Penney—But He Has Become One of the Brightest Minds in Retail," *Observer*, June 10, 2019, https://observer.com/2019/06/ron-johnscon-jc-penney-retail-guru/.

99 **Consumers' Checkbook:** Kevin Brasler and Andrea Densmore, "Sale Prices Are Rarely Real Deals," *Consumers' Checkbook*, September 6, 2023, https://www.checkbook.org/national/sale-fail/.

99 **Kohls has the audacity to say:** "LEGAL NOTICES | Kohl's," n.d., https://www.kohls.com/feature/legal-notices.jsp.

Chapter 6: Save Smarter, Not Harder

103 **Bureau of Labor Statistics takes a Consumer Expenditure Survey (CE):** U.S. Bureau of Labor Statistics, "Consumer Expenditures—2022," Bls.gov, September 8, 2023, https://www.bls.gov/news.release/cesan.nr0.htm.

105 **A 2024 study found that renting is less expensive than buying:** Alex Gailey, "Study Shows Renting Is More Affordable in the 50 Largest Metros," Bankrate, April 29, 2024, https://www.bankrate.com/real-estate/rent-vs-buy-affordability-study/.

106 **new car prices up 29 percent since March 2020:** Medora Lee, "Car Prices Are Cooling, but Should You Buy New or Used? Here Are Pros and Cons," *USA TODAY*, March 25, 2024, https://www.usatoday.com/story/money/personalfinance/2024/03/25/used-new-car-value-prices/73073720007/.

107 **the average loan for a new car is around $40K with a monthly payment of $729**: Rebecca Betterton, "Average Auto Loan Payments in 2024: What to Expect," Bankrate, May 31, 2024, https://www.bankrate.com/loans/auto-loans/average-monthly-car-payment/#stats.

Chapter 7: Simplify Your Environment

118 **University of Virginia conducted a study**: Jeff Murray, "The Bias Toward Complexity When Humans Attempt to Solve Problems," *Thomas B. Fordham Institute*, April 29, 2021, https://fordhaminstitute.org/national/commentary/bias-toward-complexity-when-humans-attempt-solve-problems.

120 **a tour of their home**: Darby E. Saxbe and Rena Repetti, "No Place Like Home: Home Tours Correlate with Daily Patterns of Mood and Cortisol," *Personality and Social Psychology Bulletin 36, no. 1* (November 23, 2009), https://doi.org/10.1177/0146167209352864.

120 **Another study found**: Lenny R. Vartanian et al., "Clutter, Chaos, and Overconsumption," *Environment and Behavior 49, no. 2* (July 27, 2016), https://doi.org/10.1177/0013916516628178.

125 **There is plenty of research**: "Stress and Health," *Nutrition Source*, Harvard T.H. Chan School of Public Health, February 2, 2023, https://www.hsph.harvard.edu/nutritionsource/stress-and-health/.

Chapter 8: Curate Your Community

137 **study conducted in the UK**: Tobias Ebert et al., "Spending Reflects Not Only *Who We Are* but Also *Who We Are Around*: The Joint Effects of Individual and Geographic Personality on Consumption," *Journal of Personality and Social Psychology 121, no. 2* (August 1, 2021), https://doi.org/10.1037/pspp0000344.

137 **thirty-year study on smoking**: Nicholas A. Christakis and James H. Fowler, "The Collective Dynamics of Smoking in a Large Social Network," *New England Journal of Medicine 358, no. 21* (May 22, 2008), https://doi.org/10.1056/nejmsa0706154.

Chapter 9: Contentment Without Complacency

155 **conducted by Empower Financial**: Kia Kokalitcheva, "A Winter Conference Heats up Finland's Startups," *Axios*, December 2, 2023, https://www.axios.com/economy/2023/12/02.

162 **needing to earn $525,000 annually**: "Can Money Buy Happiness?," *Empower*, n.d., https://www.empower.com/the-currency/money/research-financial-happiness#methodology.

162 **two researchers teamed up in an adversarial collaboration**: Matthew A. Killingsworth, Daniel Kahneman, and Barbara Mellers, "Income and

Emotional Well-being: A Conflict Resolved," *Proceedings of the National Academy of Sciences 120, no. 10* (March 1, 2023), https://doi.org/10.1073/pnas.2208661120.

163 **Federal Reserve Bank of New York:** "Household Debt and Credit Report," Federal Reserve Bank of New York, n.d., https://www.newyorkfed.org/microeconomics/hhdc.

166 **more than five million Fidelity customers:** Michelle Tessier, "Make Way for Women Investors," *Businesswire*, n.d., https://www.businesswire.com/news/home/20211008005269/en/.

Chapter 10: Big Impact Energy

173 **$2.09 trillion:** Tobias Burns and Karl Evers-Hillstrom, "Will Companies Bring Down Prices to Help Lower Inflation? So Far, Some Have 'No Regrets,'" *The Hill*, February 28, 2023, https://thehill.com/business/3876106-high-prices-are-driving-inflation/.

173 **"profit margin-led inflation":** Emily Peck, "Once a Fringe Theory, 'Greedflation' Gets Its Due," *Axios*, May 18, 2023, https://www.axios.com/2023/05/18/once-a-fringe-theory-greedflation-gets-its-due.

174 **adjusting for inflation:** Christopher Rugaber, "U.S. Consumers Keep Spending Even in the Face of Persistent Inflation and High Interest Rates," *PBS NewsHour*, October 27, 2023, https://www.pbs.org/newshour/economy/u-s-consumers-keep-spending-even-in-the-face-of-persistent-inflation-and-high-interest-rates.

174 **increased by 400 percent:** Stephanie Feldstein, "At What Cost? Unravelling the Harms of the Fast Fashion Industry," Center for Biological Diversity, n.d., https://www.biologicaldiversity.org/programs/population_and_sustainability/sustainability/fast_fashion.

174 **ends up in landfills:** Chloe Sorvino, "Food Waste Costs U.S. Taxpayers Billions of Dollars a Year," *Forbes*, July 14, 2022, https://www.forbes.com/sites/chloesorvino/2022/07/14/food-waste-costs-us-taxpayers-billions-of-dollars-a-year/.

174 **estimated $1,300 per year:** Adrienne Berard, "Study Calculates True Cost of Food Waste in America," *William & Mary*, April 20, 2020, https://www.wm.edu/news/stories/2020/study-calculates-true-cost-of-food-waste-in-america.php.

174 **more profitable than the stock market:** Juhohn Lee, "The Garbage Industry Has Outperformed the Market Since 2015. Here's Why," *CNBC*, July 22, 2021, https://www.cnbc.com/2021/07/22/how-the-garbage-industry-outperformed-the-market.html.

174 **the clothes you wear:** Emma Ross, "Fast Fashion Getting Faster: A Look at the Unethical Labor Practices Sustaining a Growing Industry," *International*

Law and Policy Brief, October 28, 2021, https://studentbriefs.law.gwu.edu /ilpb/2021/10/28/fast-fashion-getting-faster-a-look-at-the-unethical-labor -practices-sustaining-a-growing-industry/.

174 **the car you drive:** Jim Wormington, "Asleep at the Wheel," *Human Rights Watch*, February 1, 2024, https://www.hrw.org/report/2024/02/01/asleep -wheel/car-companies-complicity-forced-labor-china.

175 **11.9 billion tons of carbon dioxide:** Juan Huang et al., "Environmental Effects of China's Export Trade to the Countries along Belt and Road: An Empirical Evidence Based on Inter-Provincial Panel Data," *National Library of Medicine*, March 7, 2023, https://www.ncbi.nlm.nih.gov/pmc /articles/PMC10049068.

175 **over 40 percent of US goods:** Mark Szakonyi, "Sourcing Shift from China Pulls US Import Share to More Than a Decade Low," *IHS Markit*, February 1, 2023, https://www.spglobal.com/marketintelligence/en/mi/research -analysis/sourcing-shift-from-china-pulls-us-import-share-to-more-than-a .html.

175 **with electronics at the top:** "China Exports to United States—2024 Data 2025 Forecast 1992–2023 Historical," *Trading Economics*, n.d., https:// tradingeconomics.com/china/exports/united-states.

175 **new production by 1.39 billion phones:** Federica Laricchia, "Smart- phone Sales Worldwide 2007–2023," *Statista*, February 8, 2024, https:// www.statista.com/statistics/263437/global-smartphone-sales-to-end-users -since-2007/.

176 **Pepsi:** Michelle Chapman, "PepsiCo Profit Gets a Bump on Fewer Charges, but Sales Slip After Repeated Price Hikes," *AP News*, February 10, 2024, https://apnews.com/article/pepsico-pricefb17637f417c975c641769d 953b0112d.

176 **Walmart to lower prices:** Alice Knisley Matthias, "Walmart Is Lowering Some Grocery Prices to Pre-Inflation Levels," Allrecipes, March 1, 2024, https://www.allrecipes.com/walmart-is-lowering-grocery-prices-8603038.

Index

About the Authors

JEN SMITH is a personal finance expert and cohost of the *Frugal Friends* podcast. She and her husband paid off $78,000 of debt in two years while battling unemployment and buying a house. Jen has since become a sought-after writer and speaker, helping people live for today while being able to save for tomorrow. She's written for and been featured in top personal finance publications, including *Forbes*, *Money Magazine*, *Business Insider*, Investopedia, and more. When she's not writing or podcasting, she's training for a half-marathon at Disney World. She lives in St. Petersburg, Florida, with her husband and two sons.

JILL SIRIANNI is a licensed clinical social worker and cohost of the *Frugal Friends* podcast. She's experienced in doing a lot with a little — from starting small businesses to full-time RVing—leveraging all of it to pay off $60,000 of debt and cash-flow her master's degree. Helping others is her highest value, and integrating her mental health perspective with personal finance is how she supports others to identify and live out what they value most, what they value most. When she's not meeting with clients or podcasting, you can find her in the garden or hosting friends in her home. She lives in St. Petersburg, Florida, with her husband, Eric.